THE UNSTOPPABLE

RUTH BADER GINSBURG

THE UNSTOPPABLE
RUTH
BADER
GINSBURG

★ AMERICAN ICON ★

FOREWORD BY **MIMI LEDER**

INTRODUCTION & TEXT BY **ANTONIA FELIX**

PHOTO EDITOR **CHRISTOPHER MEASOM**

STERLING
New York

STERLING
New York

An Imprint of Sterling Publishing Co., Inc.
1166 Avenue of the Americas
New York, NY 10036

ISBN 978-1-4549-3332-8

Distributed in Canada by Sterling Publishing Co., Inc.
c/o Canadian Manda Group, 664 Annette Street
Toronto, Ontario M6S 2C8, Canada
Distributed in the United Kingdom by GMC Distribution Services
Castle Place, 166 High Street, Lewes, East Sussex BN7 1XU, England
Distributed in Australia by NewSouth Books
45 Beach Street, Coogee, NSW 2034, Australia

For information about custom editions, special sales, and premium and corporate purchases,
please contact Sterling Special Sales at 800-805-5489 or specialsales@sterlingpublishing.com.

Manufactured in Canada

sterlingpublishing.com

Interior design by Timothy Shaner, NightandDayDesign.biz

Image Credits — see page 198

Contents

Page ii: Justice Ginsburg in her chambers, Washington, DC, August 23, 2013.

Foreword
by Mimi Leder

I am not a lawyer. I am not a judicial scholar. I am a filmmaker whose life's work has been to bring aspects of the human experience to the screen, hopefully inspiring a greater understanding of our shared humanity through the power of cinematic storytelling.

I came of age in the late '60s and early '70s, a time of great promise and turbulent social upheaval in the United States. It was the birth of the Peace Corps, the National Organization for Women, and landmark legislation including the Civil Rights Act of 1964 and the Voting Rights Act of 1965; the appointment of the first African American Supreme Court Justice, Thurgood Marshall; and the historic March on Washington and Dr. Martin Luther King Jr.'s inspiring "I Have a Dream" speech.

Even as our social justice movements and human rights agendas took root and we embraced universal themes and dreams of equality, we resisted an unpopular war in Vietnam, faced the Cuban Missile Crisis, and endured the assassinations of President John F. Kennedy, Dr. King, and Robert F. Kennedy within a five-year period. We walked on the moon, but our cities and college campuses were torn apart and wrought with violence as the pain of the civil rights movement moved to the streets. Women were routinely discriminated against in wage and hiring practices and limited by established social mores reinforced by a diminished legal status—strictly on the basis of sex.

When I was accepted to the Conservatory of the American Film Institute I was twenty years old, the first woman ever admitted to the cinematography program. Much of the material I studied—in fact the history of cinema as we knew it—was told through the lens and filter of male filmmakers. Women's stories and experiences had been written and photographed by men since the creation of the medium. That said, the Golden Age of Hollywood in the 1920s brought us films through a female lens from Mary Pickford, Frances Marion, and Dorothy Arzner, and it wasn't until the '30s and '40s that the industry turned into a business driven by men. As I entered this male-dominated field

I quickly learned how many doors could be shut in my face strictly because I was a woman and how vital it was for me to follow my path. Thankfully, my father, a feminist, always told me that I could do anything, and so I did.

It was thirty-two years after my career began that I was given the opportunity to direct a movie about Ruth Bader Ginsburg, one of the most remarkable experiences of my life. Meeting Justice Ginsburg and researching the impact of her work and the obstacles she overcame gave me a new and powerful appreciation for how the opportunities and rights I enjoy stem from her work. While she had contemporaries who fought before and alongside her during the seminal judicial victories that profoundly moved the needle for women's equality, hers was a unique intellectual rigor and belief in the importance of the law not just as the foundation of our democracy, but as an instrument of *change*.

Her origin story, which inspired my film *On the Basis of Sex*, details the strategic path the young Ruth Bader Ginsburg charted, taking aim at specific discriminatory statutes and choosing her plaintiffs carefully, demonstrating that gender discrimination was harmful to women *and* men. It reveals not just the skills and legal expertise she possessed but the passion she applied to finding a path forward to change the prevalent notion that women needed to be dependent on men.

She continues, at this writing, to uphold her values on our highest court, a champion for the same principles that changed the moral compass of our nation in the last century: that all people are entitled to equal status and protection under the law. Perhaps her greatest legacy is not *just* the judicial victories that reshaped our culture. Perhaps it is the legacy of dissent and the permission, the mandate—the inalienable right—she demonstrated for *all* people to have a seat not just at the table, but also on the bench.

Some of us mirror and document the times in which we live. Some of us are fortunate enough to change the times in which we live . . . and to manifest a more just future. Justice Ginsburg's chambers, which I had the honor to visit, are decorated with an artist's rendering of the Hebrew phrase from Deuteronomy *"Tzedek, tzedek, tirdof"* (Justice, justice thou shalt pursue). On behalf of my daughters, and for all of our sons and daughters, I say to Justice Ruth Bader Ginsburg: Thank you.

—July 2018

THE UNSTOPPABLE

RUTH
BADER
GINSBURG

The Whole T(Ruth)

When a handful of Ruth Bader Ginsburg's female students at Rutgers University School of Law were trying to launch a journal about women's rights in 1971, one potential funding source called back to say no. The staffer, speaking on behalf of the directors of a major foundation, said, "They think the women's movement is a fad and will be gone in a year."

That kind of dismissal was nothing new to the women who had decided to go into the law or to Professor Ginsburg, who had started teaching at Rutgers Law in 1963 as the second woman in the faculty's fifty-five-year history. Women were only 4 percent of the profession in the early 1970s; today they make up 36 percent of American lawyers. Much of the reason they've gained that ground in the past fifty years is the women's movement—and the legal genius of Ruth Bader Ginsburg.

As a new undergraduate at Cornell, Ruth didn't foresee that she would turn the country's discriminatory laws on their head and transform society. At that point, she figured she'd be a high school history teacher. But the big story of the day in that Cold War era of the 1950s, along with the impact of one professor, changed her trajectory. Working as a research assistant for the esteemed constitutional scholar Robert Cushman, Ruth discovered the real threat behind Senator Joseph McCarthy's crusade against "card-carrying communists." As he blacklisted people in Hollywood and other industries, McCarthy's rhetoric about discussions of communism being un-American and a security threat was an attack on the First Amendment right to free speech that tore away at the country's values. The lawyers who defended the wrongly accused inspired her to look at the

Opposite: Justice Ginsburg speaks at the New York University Annual Survey of American Law dedication ceremony, April 14, 2010.

1

law in a new way. A lawyer, she observed, could do a world of good by helping to "repair tears in your community."

After graduating she married her college boyfriend, Marty Ginsburg, whom she described as the first guy she ever dated "who cared that I had a brain." They both went to Harvard Law, and, when Marty took a job in New York, Ruth finished her final year at Columbia.

Those who knew Ruth in her college and law school days saw the calm, meticulously prepared, reserved nature that would make her such a powerful force before the bench. "She seemed to have a natural ability to be logical and reasoned and not let emotions get in the way," said Irma Hilton, who attended Cornell with her. Diane Crothers, one of her students at Rutgers Law, recalled the same steady poise. "One of the things that was remarkable about her was her physical sense of self-possession," she said. "Teaching the seminar, she did not physically move her hands to gesture while she talked."

At a time when women were considered too "emotional" to be lawyers, Ruth mastered the art of calm persuasion. She had learned the fundamentals from her mother, Celia, whose intellectual prowess took second place to the family tradition of educating the oldest son. Celia taught Ruth two things: "Be a lady and be independent," Ruth said. "Be a lady meant don't give way to emotions that sap your energy, like anger. Take a deep breath and speak calmly." Those deep breaths became Ruth's trademark, thoughtful pauses.

Celia was the first child born in America to immigrant parents from Austria, and her husband, Nathan Bader, had fled Russia's anti-Jewish violence as a teenager to settle in New York. Nathan's furrier business on the Lower East Side depended on Celia's efficiency with the bookkeeping, which got them through the worst of times. Their first child, Marilyn, died from meningitis at age six, leaving one-year-old Ruth, whom Marilyn called Kiki, to grow up an only child. Ruth's passion for opera and love of the arts grew in Brooklyn with trips to

Above: Limited edition bobblehead dolls representing US Supreme Court justices (from left) David Souter, William Rehnquist, Antonin Scalia, and Ruth Bader Ginsburg.

the library, theater, concert halls and museums, and lessons on the piano and cello at home. She dreamed of becoming an opera diva, telling CNN in 2003, "If I could have any talent God could give me, I would be a great diva. But unfortunately I can only sing in the shower and in my dreams."

While teaching civil procedure as the first woman to become a tenured professor at Columbia Law School, Ruth hit her stride in the 1970s as a new breed of litigator for equal rights. Based on the spirit of the arguments that had won rights for blacks, she fought for the rights of both men and women who had been wronged simply because of their gender. Working cases through the American Civil Liberties Union Women's Rights Project—which she cofounded—Ruth spent ten years on gender discrimination cases and won five out of the six cases she argued before the United States Supreme Court.

Such wins were only possible because the time was right, she insisted. "It seemed to me that many women, at that time, were awakening to the idea that they didn't have to accept this sort of second-class treatment—this subordinate role," she said. The aim of the work those years "was to root out the gender-based classifications that riddled state and federal law books. So first you had to have a popular movement behind you. Public opinion was vitally important." She explained her mission of those years in a simple statement shortly after her eightieth birthday in 2013: "I didn't change the Constitution; the equality principle was there from the start. I just was an

66 What is the difference between a bookkeeper in New York's garment district and a Supreme Court justice? Just one generation: my mother's life and mine bear witness. Where else but America could that happen? 99

—RBG

advocate for seeing its full realization. . . . Even the Declaration of Independence starts out all men are created equal, so I see my advocacy as part of an effort to make the equality principle everything the founders would have wanted it to be if they weren't held back by the society in which they lived and particularly the shame of slavery."

Those groundbreaking years with the Women's Rights Project were followed by an appointment to a federal appeals court long considered a stepping-stone to the Supreme Court. Reflecting on President Jimmy Carter's naming her to the US Court of Appeals for the District of Columbia Circuit in 1980, Ruth credited him with wanting the court system "to reflect the talent and the knowledge of all the people of this great United States," including "minority groups and women." President Bill Clinton followed suit thirteen years later by appointing Ruth to the US Supreme Court, making her the second woman to reach the bench and the first Jewish justice in twenty-four years.

While Ruth had built a record as a moderate judge while on the DC Circuit, her lean toward the left as part of the moderate-liberal wing on the Supreme Court has won her "Notorious RBG" pop-culture status. Speaking truth to power—or "Ruth to power," as one ubiquitous meme puts it—gives her voice powerful resonance on the conservative majority court. Whether writing as part of the majority or in one of her stalwart dissents, Ruth has established her supportive stance for workers' rights, gender equity, and separation of church and state.

Through it all, Ruth's legendary achievements are wrapped in the embrace of her fifty-six-year marriage to Marty, who until his death in 2010 took her career as seriously as his own and championed her brilliance all the way to the top. Without him, she's still going strong.

At age eighty-four, legal rock star Ruth Bader Ginsburg looked back at her 1970s-era self as a "flaming feminist litigator." She had lived through the slings and arrows of gender bias as one of nine female students in a class of five hundred at Harvard Law and as an invisible, rejected job searcher after graduating (tied for first!) in her class at Columbia Law. She knew the risk of motherhood to a career—hiding her second pregnancy in oversized clothes to keep her teaching job. At eighty-five in 2018, on her twenty-fifth anniversary on the court and as the mother of two and grandmother of four, she revels in the strides her country has made toward equity and dignity for all.

Diane Crothers, one of the Rutgers Law students whom Ruth mentored at the launch of the *Women's Rights Law Reporter* in 1971, measured Ruth Bader Ginsburg's close-to-home impact in 2018. "My daughter-in-law, who is also a lawyer, was up for her last promotion while pregnant and due in two weeks. She interviewed for the promotion and got it. Boy, has the world changed."

Opposite: Oil on linen portrait of Justice Ginsburg painted in 2000 by Simmie Knox.

PART ONE

ORIGINS

Kiki's Brooklyn

If not for the overpopularity of a particular girl's name in 1930s New York, Brooklyn-born RBG would be JBG. Named Joan Ruth Bader at her birth on March 15, 1933, Joan became Ruth when her mother, Celia, enrolled her in kindergarten under her middle name to avoid confusion among the many other little Joans starting school that year. At home and among her large extended family Ruth was known by yet a third name, Kiki, pronounced "kicky," the nickname given by her older sister Marilyn for being a "kicky baby." At just one year old Kiki was too young to understand the loss of Marilyn, who at age six died from meningitis. From then on, Kiki grew up as Nathan and Celia Bader's only child, and with no memory of her sister.

Midwood, Brooklyn, was a tidy working-class haven for immigrant Jewish, Irish, and Italian families who lived in row houses and handsome brick apartment buildings. Nestled between Flatbush to the north and Coney Island to the south, the neighborhood was a quiet retreat for Ruth's father after putting in long days at his furrier shop in Manhattan. They rented the bottom of a two-story house on East 9th Street from a landlady who lived upstairs, and the sound of children playing in the street filtered in through the windows.

Opposite: Ruth Bader, August 2, 1935.

Celia was committed to exposing Ruth to the world of arts and culture just outside their doorstep, from weekly trips to the local library to Saturday plays at the Brooklyn Academy of Music. Ruth fell in love with reading at that small library situated above a Chinese restaurant, losing herself in Nancy Drew mysteries and the New England lives of Alcott's *Little Women*. The weekend performance series for children at the Brooklyn Academy of Music introduced her to everything from *Mrs. Wiggs of the Cabbage Patch* to classic film versions of Shakespeare. Celia also cultivated her musical life by starting her on piano lessons at age eight, which she continued until she was sixteen.

Ruth's Brooklyn childhood also introduced her to opera, thanks to her aunt, who brought her to a performance when she was eleven years old. Riveted by the one-hour "children's" version of the four-act opera *La Gioconda* by Ponchielli, interspersed with explanations about the plot by conductor Dean Dixon, Ruth was instantly hooked by the over-the-top drama and "gorgeous music," as she recalled. Opera music became the soundtrack of her life, and her famous passion for it would one day take her to the stage as a celebrity "extra" at the Washington National Opera (see page 160–61).

At James Madison High School, Ruth was a top student and a beautiful, popular girl who played cello in the school orchestra and cheered on the teams as a baton-twirling member of the Go-Getters Pep Club. Yet for all her popularity and sense of fun, she had a reserved, quiet intensity that was especially apparent in her careful way of speaking, punctuated with thoughtful pauses. Her honor-award achievements in confirmation class at the family's synagogue, the East Midwood Jewish Center, led to her role as rabbi at her summer camp in upstate New York, and her bright mind earned her a spot in Arista, the elite high school honor society. Simmering beneath these activities and achievements was an awareness of the gravity of life, a knowing that came at thirteen when her mother was diagnosed with cervical cancer. For the next four years she lived with "the smell of death," as she described the painful atmosphere that compounded the air of tragedy that still lingered at home after the death of her sister.

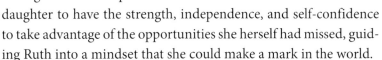

66 The Ginsburg marriage was one of those marvels of life,

a fifty-six-year marathon of love and support. 99

—Nina Totenberg

Ruth's mother, her hero, inspiration, and champion, passed away the day before Ruth's high school graduation ceremony. Instead of delivering her graduation speech, Ruth stayed home in mourning and later received her medals for her academic honors.

Celia Bader could not dream of college in her day, since that was the prize for a family's eldest son, but she channeled her intelligence and resourcefulness into her husband's business, keeping the books on track, even during the Great Depression. She raised her daughter to have the strength, independence, and self-confidence to take advantage of the opportunities she herself had missed, guiding Ruth into a mindset that she could make a mark in the world.

In the fall of 1950, Ruth began that journey by entering Cornell University in Ithaca, New York, as a government major. That first year she met Martin "Marty" David Ginsburg on a blind date and, after graduating four years later, married him at his parents' home on Long Island. She has often said that Marty was the only man she dated who was interested in her brain. "As he would later put it," wrote Ruth's friend, journalist Nina Totenberg, "she was a 'top student.' He was a 'top golfer.'" She was serious and reserved; he was outgoing and gregarious. They were perfect for each other. Throughout the next nearly six decades, their marriage would be a living example of the beliefs they shared about the equality of the sexes.

Above: Justice Ruth Bader Ginsburg (right) with her husband Martin as they listen to Justice Stephen Breyer speak at the tenth anniversary of her appointment to the Supreme Court, September 2003.

Top: Summer camp rabbi Ruth Bader delivering a sermon at Camp Che-Na-Wah in Minerva, New York, 1948. **Above**: RBG (far right), a member of the baton-wielding twirlers during her senior year at James Madison High School, Brooklyn, 1950. **Opposite**: Ruth Bader's engagement photo during her senior year at Cornell, December 1953.

❝ Marty was an extraordinary person. Of all the boys I
had dated, he was the only one who really cared that I
had a brain. And he was always—well, making me feel
that I was better than I thought I was. ❞

—RBG

Previous pages: Ruth Bader (fourth row from bottom, second from right) at the *Harvard
Law Review*, 1957. **Above left**: Martin and Ruth Ginsburg in Fort Sill, Oklahoma, 1954.
Above right: Professional bridal photograph of Ruth Bader, June 1954. **Opposite**: With
Marty at the Greenbrier resort in White Sulphur Springs, West Virginia, 1972.

"That's my dream for the world. That a child should have two caring parents who share the joys and often the burdens. It really does take a man who regards his wife as his best friend, his equal, his true partner in life."

—RBG

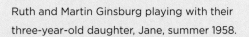

Ruth and Martin Ginsburg playing with their three-year-old daughter, Jane, summer 1958.

18

" My success in law school, I have no doubt, was in large measure because of baby Jane. I attended classes and studied diligently until four in the afternoon; the next hours were Jane's time, spent at the park, playing silly games or singing funny songs, reading picture books and A. A. Milne poems, and bathing and feeding her. After Jane's bedtime, I returned to the law books with renewed will. Each part of my life provided respite from the other and gave me a sense of proportion that classmates trained only on law studies lacked. "

—RBG

Opposite: Ruth Bader Ginsburg with her daughter, Jane, 1965.

66 *Work-life balance* was a term not yet coined in the
years my children were young; it is aptly descriptive of
the time distribution I experienced. . . . Each part of
my life provided respite from the other.99

—RBG

Opposite: The Ginsburgs on vacation (from left) Martin, Jane, James, and Ruth
at Abu Simbel, Egypt, 1985. **Above**: Sailing in the Virgin Islands, December 1980.

My Jewish Heritage

Remarks by Ruth Bader Ginsburg, US Capitol Rotunda, Washington, DC

April 22, 2004

I am pleased to join hands with all in attendance at this ceremony of remembrance. May I first express abiding appreciation to the United States Holocaust Memorial Museum for its vigilant assurance that we will never forget the victims of the Nazi madness, the six million Jews, killed simply because they were Jews, and the millions of people of other faiths and diverse affiliations swept into the unnatural maelstrom.

I had the good fortune to be a Jew born and raised in the USA. My father left Odessa bound for the New World in 1909, at age thirteen; my mother was first in her large family to be born here, in 1903, just a few months after her parents and older siblings landed in New York. What is the difference between a bookkeeper in New York's garment district and a Supreme Court justice? Just one generation, my mother's life and mine bear witness. Where else but America could that happen?

My heritage as a Jew and my occupation as a judge fit together symmetrically. The demand for justice runs through the entirety of Jewish history and Jewish tradition. I take pride in and draw strength from my heritage, as signs in my chambers attest: a large silver mezuzah on my door post, a gift from the Shulamith School for Girls in Brooklyn; on three walls, in artists' renditions of Hebrew letters, the command from Deuteronomy:

"Zedek, zedek, tirdof" (Justice, justice shall you pursue). Those words are ever-present reminders of what judges must do that they "may thrive."

But today, here in the Capitol, the lawmaking heart of our nation, in close proximity to the Supreme Court, we remember in sorrow that Hitler's Europe, his Holocaust Kingdom, was not lawless. Indeed, it was a kingdom full of laws, laws deployed by highly educated people—teachers, lawyers, and judges—to facilitate oppression, slavery, and mass murder. We convene to say "Never again," not only to Western history's most unjust regime, but also to a world in which good men and women, abroad and even in the USA, witnessed or knew of the Holocaust Kingdom's crimes against humanity, and let them happen.

The world's failure to stop the atrocities of the Third Reich was perhaps nowhere more apparent than in Hungary, where the Holocaust descended late in the war. But when it came, it advanced with brutal speed. Hungary was the first country in Europe to adopt an anti-Jewish law after World War I, a short-lived measure that restricted the admission of Jews to institutions of higher learning. In the main, however, that nation's eight hundred thousand Jews lived free from terror until 1944. Although sixty-three thousand Hungarian Jews lost their lives before the German occupation—most of them during forced service, under dreadful conditions, in labor battalions—Hungary's leaders staved off German demands to carry out the Final Solution until March 19, 1944, when Hitler's troops occupied the country.

Then, overnight, everything changed. Within three and a half months of the occupation, 437,000 Hungarian Jews were deported. Four trains a day, each transporting up to three thousand people packed together like freight, left Hungary for Auschwitz, where most of the passengers were methodically murdered. This horrendous time is chronicled unforgettably by Hungarian Holocaust survivors and Nobel Prize winners Elie Wiesel, today's lead speaker, and Imre Kertész, in their captivating works, *Night* and *Fateless*.

What happened to Hungary's Jews is a tragedy beyond reckoning. For, unlike earlier deportations, the deportations in Hungary began and relentlessly continued after the tide had turned against the Axis, and after the Nazis' crimes against humanity had been exposed. Less than a week after the German occupation of Hungary, President Roosevelt delivered a speech reporting that "the wholesale systematic murder of the Jews of Europe goes on unabated every hour" and that Hungarian Jews were now among those "threatened with annihilation." Yet, the world, for the most part, did not rise up to stop the killing.

My heritage as a Jew and my occupation as a judge fit together symmetrically. The demand for justice runs through the entirety of Jewish history and Jewish tradition.

I say "for the most part" because, as swiftly as the Hungarian Holocaust happened, heroes emerged. Raoul Wallenberg, a member of Sweden's most prominent banking family, arrived in Budapest in July 1944 and worked with the War Refugee Board—established by President Roosevelt just six months earlier—to protect tens of thousands of Jews from deportation. Wallenberg distributed Swedish protective passports; he purchased or leased buildings, draped them with Swedish flags as diplomatically immune territory, and used them as safe havens for Jews. Through these devices, he was directly responsible for saving twenty thousand people. Wallenberg carried food and medical supplies to Jews on forced marches from Budapest to Austria; he sometimes succeeded in removing Jews from the marches by insisting they were protected Swedish citizens. He has been credited with saving some one hundred thousand Jews in the Budapest ghetto by forestalling attacks on that population by Hungary's anti-Semitic Arrow Cross Party. In January 1945, Wallenberg met with Soviet officials to gain relief for the Budapest Jews. He did not return from that journey.

I am proud to live in a country where Jews are not afraid to say who we are, the second country after Israel to have set aside a day each year, this day, to remember the Holocaust, to learn of and from that era of inhumanity, to renew our efforts to repair the world's tears.

Wallenberg and the War Refugee Board are perhaps the best-known rescuers of Jews trapped in the Hungarian Holocaust. In fact, many others, Jews and Gentiles alike, also rose to the occasion. Some remain unknown for their individual deeds of heroism; others, including Carl Lutz of Switzerland, saved Jews on a larger scale. All the lifesavers were grand humans. But most of the world stood by in silence. Knowing what a few courageous souls accomplished in Hungary in short time, one can but ask: how many could have been saved throughout Europe had legions of others, both individuals and nations, the United States among them, intervened earlier?

I was fortunate to be a child, a Jewish child, safely in America during the Holocaust. Our nation learned from Hitler's racism and, in time, embarked on a mission to end law-sanctioned discrimination in our own country. In the aftermath of World War II, in the civil rights movement of the 1950s and 1960s, in the burgeoning women's rights movement of the 1970s, "We the People" expanded to include all of humankind, to embrace all the people of this great nation. Our motto, *"e pluribus unum,"* of many one, signals our appreciation that we are the richer for the religious, ethnic, and racial diversity of our citizens.

I am proud to live in a country where Jews are not afraid to say who we are, the second country after Israel to have set aside a day each year, this day, to remember the Holocaust, to learn of and from that era of inhumanity, to renew our efforts to repair the world's tears. I feel the more secure because this capital city includes a museum dedicated to educating the world, so that all may know, through proof beyond doubt, that the unimaginable in fact happened.

It is fitting, I hope you agree, as I conclude these remarks, to recite another line from Deuteronomy: *U'vacharta b'chaim.* It means "choose life." As did the survivors who somehow managed to stay alive, to carry on, and to tell their stories; as did Jews and Christians, in ghettos and in camps, who gave their lives endeavoring to save the lives of others; as did Budapest itself, where the city's Great Synagogue still opens its doors, the second largest synagogue in the world, the shul in which Theodore Herzl was bar mitzvahed, a structure so impressive visitors from my home state might recognize it as the model for Central Synagogue in New York City.

We gather here today, little more than a week after Passover, the holiday when Jews recount their journey from slavery to freedom. We retell the Passover, just as we commemorate the Holocaust, to educate our children, to remember those who died striving for a better world, and to rejoice in the resistance of the Jewish people to evil fortune, armed with the courage and faith that has enabled them to survive through centuries of exiles, plunderings, and persecutions.

The Passover story we retell is replete with miracles. But unlike our ancestors in their exodus from Egypt, our way is unlikely to be advanced by miraculous occurrences. In striving to drain dry the waters of prejudice and oppression, we must rely on measures of our own creation—upon the wisdom of our laws and the decency of our institutions, upon our reasoning minds and our feeling hearts. And as a constant spark to carry on, upon our vivid memories of the evils we wish to banish from our world. In our long struggle for a more just world, our memories are among our most powerful resources.

May the memory of those who perished remain vibrant to all who dwell in this fair land, people of every color and creed. May that memory strengthen our resolve to aid those at home and abroad who suffer from injustice born of ignorance and intolerance, to combat crimes that stem from racism and prejudice, and to remain ever engaged in the quest for democracy and respect for the human dignity of all the world's people.

Above: Justice Ruth Bader Ginsburg, the first Jewish woman to be appointed to the Supreme Court, talks with filmmaker David Grubin about his PBS series *The Jewish Americans*, January 10, 2008, in Washington. **Following pages**: American Jewish diaspora (from left to right) Lauren Bacall, Dr. Ruth Westheimer, Larry Tish, Preston Tish, Itzhak Perlman, Arthur Miller, Mark Spitz, The Honorable Ruth Bader Ginsburg, Philip Glass, Ed Koch, Betty Friedan, Ralph Lauren, Isaac Stern, Ellis Island, New York, 1996.

66 When I announced her appointment, she spoke about her grandchildren. Someday, I believe my grandchildren will benefit from and learn from the contributions she is about to make. 99

—President Bill Clinton

Above: Chief Justice William Rehnquist (far right) swearing in the newest member of the Supreme Court as President Bill Clinton (left) and Ruth Bader Ginsburg's husband, Martin Ginsburg, look on, August 10, 1993. **Opposite**: The first day on the job: (from left) son-in-law George Spera, daughter Jane Ginsburg, husband Martin, son James Ginsburg, and (in front) grandchildren Clara and Paul Spera, October 1, 1993.

" I have had more than a little bit of luck in life, but nothing equals in magnitude my marriage to Martin D. Ginsburg. I do not have words adequate to describe my super smart, exuberant, ever-loving spouse. Early on in our marriage, it became clear to him that cooking was not my strong suit. To the eternal appreciation of our food-loving children (we became four in 1965, when our son, James, was born), Marty made the kitchen his domain and became chef supreme in our home. Marty coached me through the birth of our son, he was the first reader and critic of articles, speeches and briefs I drafted, and he was at my side constantly, in and out of the hospital, during two long bouts with cancer. And I betray no secret in reporting that, without him, I would not have gained a seat on the Supreme Court. "

—RBG

Prominent tax attorney and husband of Supreme Court nominee, Martin Ginsburg, at their Watergate apartment, Washington, DC, July 1993.

PART TWO

BREAKING BARRIERS

Steel Butterfly

Like true soul mates, Ruth and Marty Ginsburg decided in college to pursue the same profession so that they could spend the rest of their lives engaged with and supportive of each other's work and ideas. When they ultimately agreed upon law as that field, Marty entered Harvard Law School and Ruth, with her impressive academic standing as the woman with the highest grades in her class at Cornell, also won admission and a scholarship. After she and Marty were married, Marty was drafted into the reserves and they put law school on hold for two years. During that time, Ruth gave birth to their first child, Jane, in the summer of 1955. Upon their return from Marty's base in Oklahoma, Ruth entered Harvard Law—one of only nine female students in a class of five hundred—and Marty began year two. It would be a year like no other.

That first semester in 1956, Marty was diagnosed with testicular cancer and given a dire prognosis. As he endured months of surgeries and radiation treatments, Ruth continuously gathered and organized notes from his classmates, cared for him and their baby, and kept up with her own classes. Miraculously, the nightmarish school year ended with victories on all sides. Marty passed

Opposite: At incoming secretary of state Condoleezza Rice's swearing-in ceremony, Washington, DC, January 28, 2005.

his courses with strong grades. Ruth passed with *stellar* grades as one of the top ten students in the class and aced the rigorous end-of-first-year writing competition to make law review, a feat her husband had not achieved. But Marty had his own win, beating all the odds to finish the year cancer-free.

When the young family moved to New York City for Marty's new job at a top law firm, Ruth spent her final year of law school at Columbia University and graduated in a tie for first in her class. To the legal world, however, she seemed invisible. Any man with her record would have been invited to clerk at the Supreme Court or an appellate court or offered a job at a distinguished firm, but no one was interested in Ruth. She later reflected about the three strikes inflicted upon her during that discouraging time. "In the fifties, the traditional law firms were just beginning to turn around on hiring Jews," she wrote. "But to be a woman, a Jew and a mother to boot—that combination was a bit too much."

Joining the faculty of Rutgers School of Law in 1963, Ruth became the second female law professor in the school's history and began the sex discrimination work with which she would change American society. As she took on discrimination cases for the American Civil Liberties Union, she chipped away at the overt gender barriers in the law. The job, she said, was to get rid of the "separate spheres" mentality in the law, the notion that "men were the doers in the world and women were the stay-at-home types." That ingrained mentality, in fact, forced her to hide her pregnancy in oversized clothes in 1965 to ensure that the dean would offer her another contract for the next year.

66 We had nearly two whole years far from school, far from career pressures and far from relatives, to learn about each other and begin to build a life. 99

—Martin Ginsburg

The highlight of Ruth's beginnings with the ACLU was *Reed v. Reed*, in which Sally Reed was fighting the Idaho law that gave men the sole right to administer dead people's estates. Ruth's goal in her brief to the Supreme Court (she did not argue the case) was to persuade the court that gender, like race, should be subjected to the highest standard of review; in other words, the highest court in the land should take a more skeptical look at the constitutionality of sex-based laws. Her detailed brief outlined the "legally enforced second-class status of women and pointed to the historical analogy between the political, social, and legal status of women and that of African Americans," wrote legal scholar Wendy W. Williams. Treat sex like race, Ruth demanded, and clear

away laws that create barriers for women. With this brief, Ruth was the first lawyer to bring this argument to the Supreme Court, and the court ruled in favor of Sally Reed. The landmark decision did not equate sex with race, but it did strike down the Idaho law, and from that day forward, "the days of assuming automatically that women were different from the standard citizen were over," wrote Linda Hirshman in *Sisters in Law*.

Ruth's ACLU work intensified after she joined the Columbia University School of Law faculty in 1972 and cofounded the ACLU Women's Rights Project. The obstacles she had faced as a woman, mother, and Jew steeled her drive as she handled groundbreaking cases through the 1970s, always keeping the calm, steady, "lady's" composure her mother had instilled in her. "She's sort of a steel butterfly," said her former colleague Vivian Berger. "She's gone through a lot. She never whines about it, but she makes sure people know what it was like."

Above: Professor Ginsburg, Columbia Law School, 1980.

66 It takes women and men who are feminists. By feminists I mean people who think women should have equal chances to do whatever their talent permits them to do. They have to be willing to ask for these accommodations. It's more than asking—it's expecting how workplaces should be organized. 99

—RBG

Opposite: Ruth Bader Ginsburg while scholar in residence at the Rockefeller Foundation in Italy, summer 1977. **Above**: Ruth Bader Ginsburg in New York, 1972, the year she was named a professor at Columbia Law School.

66 I was terribly nervous. In fact, I didn't eat lunch for fear that I might throw up. Two minutes into my argument, the fear dissolved. Suddenly, I realized that here before me were the nine leading jurists of America, a captive audience. I felt a surge of power that carried me through. 🙷🙷

—RBG, describing the first time she argued
before the Supreme Court

Above: Professor Ginsburg, Columbia Law, 1975.
Opposite: In her apartment, New York, 1977.

Let's Take It!

(or How the 10th Circuit Court of Appeals Got My Wife Her Good Job)

A Speech by Martin D. Ginsburg (delivered by Justice Ginsburg after his death), the 10th Circuit Court of Appeals Annual Conference, Colorado Springs, Colorado

August 27, 2010

As you have heard, my field is tax law. When Chief Judge Henry asked me to speak today and hinted it might be on my favorite subject, naturally I prepared a long paper addressing the Supreme Court's performance in tax cases. Sadly, the chief judge reacted with surprising hostility and so I am going to speak instead about the only significant thing I have done in my long life with Honorable Ruth. I shall recall for you the one case in which we served as co-counsel. It was also the one occasion either of us was privileged to argue in the 10th Circuit. Nonetheless, fascinating as you will surely find this reminiscence, all in all you are the losers, for I promise you, the Supreme Court's performance in tax cases is an exceedingly funny subject.

In the 1960s I practiced law, mainly tax law, in New York City, and Ruth began her law teaching career at Rutgers Law School in Newark. One of the courses she taught was Constitutional Law, and, toward the end of the decade, she started looking into equal protection issues that might be presented by statutes that differentiate on the basis of sex. A dismal academic undertaking because, back then, the United States Supreme Court had never invalidated any legislative classification that differentiated on the basis of sex.

Then as now, at home Ruth and I worked evenings in adjacent rooms. Her room is bigger. In my little room one evening in fall 1970, I was reading tax court advance sheets and came upon a pro se litigant, one Charles E. Moritz, who, on a stipulated record, was denied a $600 dependent care deduction under old section 214 of the Internal Revenue Code, even though, the tax court found, the operative facts—save one—fit the statute perfectly. Mr. Moritz was an editor and traveling salesman for a book company. His eighty-nine-year-old dependent mother lived with him. In order to be gainfully employed without neglecting Mother or packing her off to an old-age home, Charles paid an unrelated individual at least $600—in fact, a good deal more than that—to take care of his mother when he was away at work.

There was just one small problem, and in the tax court, it served to do him in. The statute awarded its up-to-$600 deduction to a taxpayer who was a woman of any classification (divorced, widowed, or single), a married couple, a widowed man, or a divorced man. But not to a single man who had never been married. Mr. Moritz was a single man who had never married. "Deductions are a matter of legislative grace," the tax court quoted, and added that if the taxpayer were raising a constitutional objection, forget about it: everyone knows, the tax court confidently asserted, that the Internal Revenue Code is immune from constitutional attack.

Let me digress a moment to tell you that in the tax court Mr. Moritz, although not a lawyer, had written a brief. It was one page in length and said: "If I were a dutiful daughter instead of a dutiful son, I would have received the deduction. This makes no sense." It was from that brief the tax court gleaned the taxpayer might be raising a constitutional objection. Mr. Moritz's one-page submission remains in my mind as the most persuasive brief I ever read.

Well, I went to the big room next door, handed the tax court advance sheets to my spouse, and said, "Read this." Ruth replied with a warm and friendly snarl, "I don't read tax cases." I said, "Read this one," and returned to my little room.

No more than five minutes later—it was a short opinion—Ruth stepped into my little room and, with the broadest smile you can imagine, said, "Let's take it!" And we did.

> If the taxpayer were raising a constitutional objection, forget about it: everyone knows, the tax court confidently asserted, that the Internal Revenue Code is immune from constitutional attack.

Ruth and I took the Moritz appeal pro bono of course, but since the taxpayer was not indigent we needed a pro bono organization. We thought of the American Civil Liberties Union. Mel Wulf, the ACLU's then legal director, naturally wished to review our proposed 10th Circuit brief, which in truth was 90 percent Ruth's 10th Circuit brief. When Mel read the brief, he was greatly persuaded.

A few months later, the ACLU had its first sex discrimination/equal protection case in the United States Supreme Court. As many of you will recall, it was titled *Reed v. Reed*. Remembering Moritz, Mel asked Ruth if she would take the lead in writing the ACLU's Supreme Court brief on behalf of appellant Sally Reed. Ruth did and, reversing the decision of the Idaho Supreme Court, the US Supreme Court unanimously held for Sally.

Good for Sally Reed and good for Ruth, who decided thereafter to hold down two jobs, one as a tenured professor at Columbia Law School, where she had moved from Rutgers; the other as head of the ACLU's newly created Women's Rights Project.

Now back to *Moritz*. The 10th Circuit—Judge Holloway writing for the panel—found Mr. Moritz to have been denied the law's equal protection, reversed the tax court, and allowed Mr. Moritz his $600 deduction.

Amazingly, the government petitioned for certiorari. The 10th Circuit's decision, the government asserted, cast a cloud of unconstitutionality over literally hundreds of federal statutes—laws that, like old section 214 of the tax code, differentiated solely on the basis of sex.

In those pre–personal computer days, there was no easy way for us to test the government's assertion. But Solicitor General Erwin Griswold took care of that by attaching to his cert. petition a list—generated by the Department of Defense's mainframe computer—of those hundreds of suspect federal statutes. Cert. was denied in Moritz, and the computer list proved a gift beyond price. Over the balance of the decade, in Congress, the Supreme

Court, and many other courts, Ruth successfully urged the unconstitutionality of those statutes.

So our trip to the 10th Circuit mattered a lot. First, it fueled Ruth's early 1970s career shift from diligent academic to enormously skilled and successful appellate advocate—which in turn led to her next career on the higher side of the bench. Second, with Dean Griswold's help, Mr. Moritz's case furnished the litigation agenda Ruth actively pursued until she joined the DC Circuit in 1980.

All in all, great achievements from a tax case with an amount in controversy that totaled exactly $296.70.

As you can see, in bringing those tax court advance sheets to Ruth's big room forty years ago, I changed history. For the better. And, I shall claim, thereby rendered a significant service to the nation. I have decided to believe it is the significant service that led to my being invited to speak to you today. And even if you had in mind a topic a little less cosmically significant and substantially more humorous, such as the Supreme Court's performance in tax cases, Ruth and I are truly delighted to be back with you in the 10th Circuit once again.

Opposite: Ruth Bader Ginsburg, 1977.

❝ I was trying to educate the judges that there was something wrong with the notion 'Sugar and spice and everything nice, that's what little girls are made of'—for that very notion was limiting the opportunities, the aspirations of our daughters.❞

—RBG

Above: President Jimmy Carter shaking hands with Judge Ruth Bader Ginsburg at a reception for the National Association of Women's Judges at the White House, October 3, 1980. **Opposite**: Portrait of first-term DC Circuit judge Ruth Bader Ginsburg, 1980.

Half the Talent Pool

Ruth Bader Ginsburg's US Supreme Court Justice Nomination Acceptance Address,
White House Rose Garden, Washington, DC

June 14, 1993

I am grateful beyond measure for the confidence you have placed in me, and I will strive with all that I have to live up to your expectations in making this appointment.

I appreciate, too, the special caring of Senator Daniel Patrick Moynihan, the more so because I do not actually know the senator. I was born and brought up in New York, the state Senator Moynihan represents, and he was the very first person to call with good wishes when President Carter nominated me in 1980 to serve on the US Court of Appeals for the District of Columbia Circuit. Senator Moynihan has offered the same encouragement on this occasion.

May I introduce at this happy moment three people very special to me: my husband, Martin D. Ginsburg; my son-in-law, George T. Spera Jr.; and my son, James Steven Ginsburg.

The announcement the president just made is significant, I believe, because it contributes to the end of the days when women, at least half the talent pool in our society, appear in high places only as one-at-a-time performers. Recall that when

President Carter took office in 1976, no woman had ever served on the Supreme Court, and only one woman, Shirley Hufstedler of California, then served at the next federal court level, the United States Courts of Appeals.

Today, Justice Sandra Day O'Connor graces the Supreme Court bench, and close to twenty-five women serve at the Federal Court of Appeals level, two as chief judges. I am confident that more will soon join them. That seems to me inevitable, given the change in law school enrollment.

My law school class in the late 1950s numbered over five hundred. That class included less than ten women. As the president said, not a law firm in the entire city of New York bid for my employment as a lawyer when I earned my degree. Today few law schools have female enrollment under 40 percent, and several have reached or passed the 50 percent mark. And thanks to Title VII, no entry doors are barred.

My daughter, Jane, reminded me a few hours ago in a good-luck call from Australia of a sign of the change we have had the good fortune to experience. In her high school yearbook on her graduation in 1973, the listing for Jane Ginsburg under "ambition" was "to see her mother appointed to the Supreme Court." The next line read, "If necessary, Jane will appoint her." Jane is so pleased, Mr. President, that you did it instead, and her brother, James, is, too.

I expect to be asked in some detail about my views of the work of a good judge on a high court bench. This afternoon is not the moment for extended remarks on that subject, but I might state a few prime guides.

I pray that I may be all that she would have been had she lived in an age when women could aspire and achieve and daughters are cherished as much as sons.

Chief Justice Rehnquist offered one I keep in the front of my mind: a judge is bound to decide each case fairly in a court with the relevant facts and the applicable law even when the decision is not—as he put it—what the home crowd wants.

Next, I know no better summary than the one Justice O'Connor recently provided drawn from a paper by New York University Law School professor Burt Neuborne. The remarks concern the enduring influence of Justice Oliver Wendell Holmes. They read: "When a modern constitutional judge is confronted with a hard case, Holmes is at her side with three gentle reminders: first, intellectual honesty about the available policy choices; second, disciplined self-restraint in respecting the majority's policy choice; and third, principled commitment to defense of individual autonomy even in the face of majority action."

To that I can only say, "Amen."

I am indebted to so many for this extraordinary chance and challenge: to a revived women's movement in the 1970s that opened doors for people like me, to the civil rights movement of the 1960s from which the women's movement drew inspiration, to my teaching colleagues at Rutgers and Columbia and for thirteen years my DC Circuit colleagues who shaped and heightened my appreciation of the value of collegiality.

Most closely, I have been aided by my life partner, Martin D. Ginsburg, who has been, since our teenage years, my best friend and biggest booster; by my mother-in-law, Evelyn Ginsburg, the most supportive parent a person could have; and by a daughter and son with the tastes to appreciate that Daddy cooks ever so much better than Mommy and so phased me out of the kitchen at a relatively early age.

Finally, I know Hillary Rodham Clinton has encouraged and supported the president's decision to utilize the skills and talents of all the people of the United States. I did not, until today, know

Mrs. Clinton, but I hasten to add that I am not the first member of my family to stand close to her.

There is another I love dearly to whom the First Lady is already an old friend. My wonderful granddaughter, Clara, witnessed this super, unposed photograph taken last October when Mrs. Clinton visited the nursery school in New York and led the little ones in "The Toothbrush Song." The small person right in front is Clara.

I have a last thank-you. It is to my mother, Celia Amster Bader, the bravest and strongest person I have known, who was taken from me much too soon. I pray that I may be all that she would have been had she lived in an age when women could aspire and achieve and daughters are cherished as much as sons.

I look forward to stimulating weeks this summer and, if I am confirmed, to working at a neighboring court to the best of my ability for the advancement of the law in the service of society.

Thank you.

Above: Nominee Ginsburg during her acceptance speech in the White House Rose Garden showing a picture of Hillary Rodham Clinton reading to her granddaughter's nursery school class, June 14, 1993.

Above: Supreme Court nominee Ginsburg making the rounds on Capitol Hill before the judiciary committee hearings. With Senator Joe Biden, a Democrat and chairman of the Senate Judiciary Committee (top), and with the ranking Republican of the Senate Judiciary Committee, Senator Orrin Hatch (below), June 15, 1993. **Opposite**: In the office of Senator Strom Thurmond, June 16, 1993.

The Most Awesome Trust

Prepared Statement of Judge Ginsburg [abridged], Hearings before the
United States Senate Committee on the Judiciary, Washington, DC

July 20, 1993

I am, as you know from my responses to your questionnaire, a Brooklynite born and bred—a first-generation American on my father's side, barely second generation on my mother's. Neither of my parents had the means to attend college, but both taught me to love learning, to care about people, and to work hard for whatever I wanted or believed in. Their parents had the foresight to leave the old country when Jewish ancestry and faith meant exposure to pogroms and denigration of one's human worth. What has become of me could happen only in America. Like so many others, I owe so much to the entry this nation afforded to people "yearning to breathe free."

I have had the great fortune to share life with a partner truly extraordinary for his generation, a man who believed at age eighteen, when we met, and who believes today that a woman's work—at home or on the job—is as important as a man's. I became a lawyer in days when women were not wanted by most members of the legal profession, because Marty and his parents supported that choice unreservedly.

I have been deeply moved by the outpouring of good wishes received in recent weeks from fam-

ily, neighbors, campmates, classmates, students at Rutgers and Columbia, law-teaching colleagues, lawyers with whom I have worked, judges across the country, and many women and men who do not know me. That huge, spirit-lifting collection shows that for many of our people, an individual's sex is no longer remarkable or even unusual with regard to his or her qualifications to serve on the Supreme Court.

Indeed, in my lifetime, I expect to see three, four, and perhaps even more women on the high court bench, women not shaped from the same mold, but of different complexions. Yes, there are still miles in front, but what a distance we have traveled from the day President Thomas Jefferson told his secretary of state: "The appointment of women to [public] office is an innovation for which the public is not prepared. Nor," Jefferson added, "am I."

The increasingly full use of the talent of all of this nation's people holds large promise for the future, but we could not have come to this point—and I surely would not be in this room today—without the determined efforts of men and women who kept dreams of equal citizenship alive in days when few would listen. People like Susan B. Anthony, Elizabeth Cady Stanton, and Harriet Tubman come to mind. I stand on the shoulders of those brave people.

Indeed, in my lifetime, I expect to see three, four, and perhaps even more women on the high court bench, women not shaped from the same mold, but of different complexions.

Supreme Court justices are guardians of the great charter that has served as our nation's fundamental instrument of government for over two hundred years, the oldest written Constitution still in force in the world. But the justices do not guard constitutional rights alone. Courts share that profound responsibility with the Congress, the president, the states, and the people. Constant realization of a more perfect union, the Constitution's aspiration, requires the widest, broadest, deepest participation on matters of government and government policy.

One of the world's greatest jurists, Judge Learned Hand, said that the spirit of liberty that imbues our Constitution must lie, first and foremost, in the hearts of the men and women who compose this great nation. He defined that spirit, in a way I fully embrace, as one which is not too sure that it is right, and so seeks to understand the minds of other men and women and to weigh the interests of others alongside its own without bias. The spirit Judge Learned Hand described strives for a community where the least shall be heard and considered side by side with the greatest. I will keep that wisdom in the front of my mind as long as I am capable of judicial service.

Some of you asked me, during recent visits, why I want to be on the Supreme Court. It is an opportunity, beyond any other, for one of my training to serve society. The controversies that come to the Supreme Court, as the last judicial resort, touch and concern the health and well-being of our nation and its people; they affect the preservation of liberty to ourselves and our posterity. Serving on this court is the highest honor, the most awesome trust that can be placed in a judge. It means working at my craft—working with and for the law—as a way to keep our society both ordered and free.

Let me try to state in a nutshell how I view the work of judging. My approach, I believe, is neither liberal nor conservative. Rather, it is rooted in the place of the judiciary—of judges—in our democratic society. The Constitution's preamble speaks first of "We, the People," and then of their elected representatives. The judiciary is third in line, and it is placed apart from the political fray so that its members can judge fairly, impartially, in accordance with the law and without fear about the animosity of any pressure group.

In Alexander Hamilton's words, the mission of judges is "to secure a steady, upright, and impartial administration of the laws." I would add that the judge should carry out that function without fanfare, but with due care. She should decide the case before her without reaching out to cover cases not yet seen. She should be ever mindful, as Judge and then Justice Benjamin Nathan Cardozo said: "Justice is not to be taken by storm. She is to be wooed by slow advances."

We—this committee and I—are about to embark on many hours of conversation. You have arranged this hearing to aid you in the performance of a vital task—to prepare your Senate colleagues for consideration of my nomination.

The record of the Constitutional Convention shows that the delegates had initially entrusted the power to appoint federal judges, most prominently, Supreme Court justices, not to the president, but to you and your colleagues—to the Senate, acting alone. Only in the waning days of the convention did the framers settle on a nomination role for the president and an advise and consent role for the Senate.

The text of the Constitution, as finally formulated, makes no distinction between the appointment process for Supreme Court justices and the process for other officers of the United States, for example, cabinet officers. But as history bears out, you and senators past have sensibly considered appointments in relation to the appointee's task.

In Alexander Hamilton's words, the mission of judges is "to secure a steady, upright, and impartial administration of the laws."

Federal judges may long outlast the president who appoints them. They may serve as long as they can do the job, as the Constitution says, they may remain in office "during good Behaviour." Supreme Court justices, particularly, participate in shaping a lasting body of constitutional decisions; they continuously confront matters on which the Framers left many things unsaid, unsettled, or uncertain. For that reason, when the Senate considers a Supreme Court nomination, the senators

Opposite: Testifying before the Senate Judiciary Committee on Tuesday, July 20, 1993.

are properly concerned about the nominee's capacity to serve the nation, not just for the here and now, but over the long term.

You have been supplied, in the five weeks since the president announced my nomination, with hundreds of pages about me, and thousands of pages I have penned—my writings as a law teacher, mainly about procedure; ten years of briefs filed when I was a courtroom advocate of the equal stature of men and women before the law; numerous speeches and articles on that same theme; thirteen years of opinions—well over seven hundred of them—decisions I made as a member of the US Court of Appeals for the District of Columbia Circuit; several comments on the roles of judges and lawyers in our legal system. That body of material, I know, has been examined by the committee with care. It is the most tangible, reliable indicator of my attitude, outlook, approach, and style. I hope you will judge my qualifications principally on that written record spanning thirty-four years, and that you will find in it assurance that I am prepared to do the hard work and to exercise the informed and independent judgment that Supreme Court decision making entails.

I think of these proceedings much as I do of the division between the written record and briefs, on the one hand, and oral argument, on the other hand, in appellate tribunals. The written record is by far the more important component in an appellate court's decision making, but the oral argument often elicits helpful clarifications and concentrates

the judges' minds on the character of the decision they are called upon to make.

There is, of course, this critical difference. You are well aware that I came to this proceeding to be judged as a judge, not as an advocate. Because I am and hope to continue to be a judge, it would be wrong for me to say or preview in this legislative chamber how I would cast my vote on questions the Supreme Court may be called upon to decide. Were I to rehearse here what I would say and how I would reason on such questions, I would act injudiciously.

> A judge sworn to decide impartially can offer no forecasts, no hints, for that would not only show disregard for the specifics of the particular case; it would display disdain for the entire judicial process.

Judges in our system are bound to decide concrete cases, not abstract issues; each case is based on particular facts, and its decision should turn on those facts and the governing law, stated and explained in light of the particular arguments the parties or their representatives choose to present. A judge sworn to decide impartially can offer no forecasts, no hints, for that would not only show disregard for the specifics of the particular case; it would display disdain for the entire judicial process.

Similarly, because you are considering my capacity for independent judging, my personal views on how I would vote on a publicly debated issue were I in your shoes—were I a legislator—are not what you will be closely examining. As Justice Oliver Wendell Holmes counseled: "[O]ne of the most sacred duties of a judge is not to read [her] convictions into [the C]onstitution." I have tried, and I will continue to try, to follow the model Justice Holmes set in holding that duty sacred.

I see this hearing, as I know you do, as a grand opportunity once again to reaffirm that civility, courtesy, and mutual respect properly keynote our exchanges. Judges, I am mindful, owe the elected branches—the Congress and the president—respectful consideration of how court opinions affect their responsibilities. And I am heartened by legislative branch reciprocal sensitivity. As one of you said two months ago at a meeting of the Federal Judges Association: "We in Congress must be more thoughtful and deliberate in order to enable judges to do their job more effectively."

As for my own deportment or, in the Constitution's words, "good Behaviour," I prize advice received on this nomination from a dear friend, Frank Griffin, a recently retired justice of the Supreme Court of Ireland. Justice Griffin wrote: "Courtesy to and consideration for one's colleagues, the legal profession, and the public are among the greatest attributes a judge can have."

It is fitting, as I conclude this opening statement, to express my deep respect for and abid-

ing appreciation to Justice Byron R. White for his thirty-one years and more of fine service on the Supreme Court. In acknowledging his colleagues' good wishes on the occasion of his retirement, Justice White wrote that he expects to sit on US Courts of Appeals from time to time, and so to be a consumer of, instead of a participant in, Supreme Court opinions. He expressed a hope shared by all lower court judges; he hoped "the [Supreme] Court's mandates will be clear [and] crisp,...[leaving] as little room as possible for disagreement about their meaning. If confirmed, I will take the counsel to heart and strive to write opinions that both "get it right" and "keep it tight."

Above: Testifying before the Senate Judiciary Committee, July 20, 1993. **Following pages**: Greeting her husband, Martin, as she introduces her family during the hearings. The Ginsburgs' son, James, and his wife, Lisa Brauston, are at left.

66 Generally, change in our society is incremental, I think. Real change,

enduring change, happens one step at a time. 99

—RBG

Above and **Opposite**: President Bill Clinton and the newly confirmed
(by a vote of 96–3) Supreme Court justice Ruth Bader Ginsburg speak
to the press in the White House Rose Garden, August 3, 1993.

PART THREE

MAKING HER CASE

Reason to Hope

Throughout the 1970s, Ruth successfully challenged laws that blocked people's rights simply based on their gender. Those laws worked both ways: some discriminated against women and some—as she was the first to point out—brought a disadvantage to men.

In 1972, she and Marty famously teamed up to battle sexism in a case involving a man in his sixties who wanted the tax deduction for taking care of a disabled relative, his elderly mother.

The IRS denied the deduction, claiming that it was only available to a woman, not a man. Resting on this stereotype that only women are caregivers, the IRS had drawn a line that needed to be erased. Ruth and Marty argued *Moritz v. Commissioner of Internal Revenue* in the 10th Circuit Court of Appeals and won for Charles Moritz (see pages 44–46).

Over the next several years, Ruth led the march (without her twirling baton) to battle legalized sexism and successfully argued five out of six landmark cases before the Supreme Court. These wins changed everything, establishing the modern law of equal protection in terms of gender equality.

Opposite: Posing beneath a portrait of Chief Justice Rehnquist in the West Conference Room of the Supreme Court on her twentieth anniversary on the job, August 30, 2013.

Her cases convinced the court, for example, that a female air force lieutenant deserved the same benefits as a male member of the force (*Frontiero v. Richardson*, 1973) and that male Oklahoma bar-goers had the right to drink at the same age as young women (*Craig v. Boren*, 1976). Great social strides came in the big picture–shift cases like these made in the nation's psyche: Ruth said that *Craig* showed the court that the "familiar stereotype: the active boy, aggressive and assertive; the passive girl, docile and submissive" was "not fit to be written into law."

A decade of history-making work brought Ruth to the attention of President Jimmy Carter, and she traded in her professor's hat and robe for those of a judge. As a judge on the US Court of Appeals for the District of Columbia, or DC Circuit, Ruth joined a bench traditionally seen as a stepping-stone to the US Supreme Court. (Four current Supreme Court justices came from the DC Circuit: Chief Justice John Roberts, Clarence Thomas, Elena Kagan, and RBG.)

The DC Circuit holds a special place in the system since it handles challenges to regulations and other actions taken by federal agencies—issues that affect everyone. Taking the bench in 1980, forty-seven-year-old Ruth would develop a reputation as a moderate judge who could find consensus with even the most conservative members of the bench, including Antonin Scalia, who became a close friend.

Once settled into their Washington apartment at the Watergate, Marty's cooking talents became the talk of the town. "He wasn't just a great chef," Ruth said. "He really was stupendous, and at the same time that he was one of the country's leading tax experts and one of the funniest men alive."

After thirteen years on the DC Circuit, Ruth appeared on President Bill Clinton's shortlist of nominees to the US Supreme Court, and Marty leapt into action to gather support from powerful figures throughout his network—just as he had done when Ruth was nominated for the DC Circuit. As a result, Ruth became President Clinton's pick, passed her Senate hearing by a vote of 96–3, and was sworn in on August 10, 1993.

66 One of her favorite things to do was to always show the double-edged sword of everything. She had a flair for knowing what kind of nonlegal but relevant social and historical facts needed to be put into a brief to get the justices to understand. 99

—Brenda Feigen, a lawyer who worked with Ginsburg on
Frontiero at the Women's Rights Project

At age sixty Ruth became the 107th person and second woman (after Sandra Day O'Connor) to ascend to the country's highest court. One of the most essential rulings Ruth has made on the Court came in her third year, *United States v. Virginia*, involving the Virginia Military Institute's all-male admissions policy. Ruth wrote the majority opinion, which held that VMI's policy violated the Fourteenth Amendment's equal protection clause.

Ruth's dissents became legendary for their sting and her untraditional practice of sometimes reading them from the bench. In *Bush v. Gore* (2000), in which the court halted the Florida presidential election recount, Ruth famously dissented without including the typical polite "respectfully" before the word "dissent." In 2014, her dissent about the court's 5–4 Hobby Lobby Stores decision went viral on the internet as the country weighed in on this hotly controversial case. According to Ruth, by allowing a company to deny insurance coverage for birth control on religious grounds, "The court, I fear, has ventured into a minefield."

As one of the most venerated women in American public life, Ruth's perspective and insights—on the law and otherwise—are in demand among all ages. After the Women's Marches following the 2017 inauguration of President Donald Trump, in which millions of people expressed their "dissent" over the president's views, she was inspired by the size and peacefulness of the demonstrations. "We are not experiencing the best times," she said, "but there is reason to hope that we will see a better day."

Opposite: In the justices' dining room, October 1, 1993. **Above**: Chief Justice William Rehnquist walks down the steps of the courthouse with the Supreme Court's newest member her first day on the job, Friday, October 1, 1993.

"It is true, as Jeanne Coyne of Minnesota's Supreme Court famously said: At the end of the day, a wise old man and a wise old woman will reach the same decision. But it is also true that women, like persons of different racial groups and ethnic origins, contribute what the late Fifth Circuit judge Alvin Rubin, described as 'a distinctive medley of views influenced by differences in biology, cultural impact, and life experience.' Our system of justice is surely richer for the diversity of background and experience of its judges. It was poorer when nearly all of its participants were cut from the same mold."

—RBG

Sandra Day O'Connor with Ruth Bader Ginsburg—the only two female justices of the US Supreme Court at the time—in Statuary Hall before addressing a meeting of the Congressional Women's Caucus, March 28, 2001.

66 When I began teaching law in 1963 . . . law school textbooks in that decade contained such handy advice as 'land, like woman, was meant to be possessed.' 99

—RBG

Above: Sandra Day O'Connor and Ruth Bader Ginsburg onstage at the Opera House celebrating the birthday of Michael Kaiser, president of the Kennedy Center, October 27, 2003. **Opposite**: Supreme Court justices watch four-year-old Jack Roberts (lower right), the son of Judge John Roberts, fidget in his chair while his father is sworn in as the seventeenth chief justice of the United States in the East Room of the White House. (Front to back) are Justices Sandra Day O'Connor, Anthony Kennedy, David Souter, Clarence Thomas, and Ruth Bader Ginsburg, Thursday, September 29, 2005.

Above and **Opposite top**: In her chambers at the Supreme Court and with her clerks, August 2002. **Opposite below**: (from left to right) Justices Stephen Breyer, Ruth Bader Ginsburg, Clarence Thomas, John Paul Stevens, and John Roberts react to an amusing anecdote during a memorial for the late chief justice William H. Rehnquist, 2006.

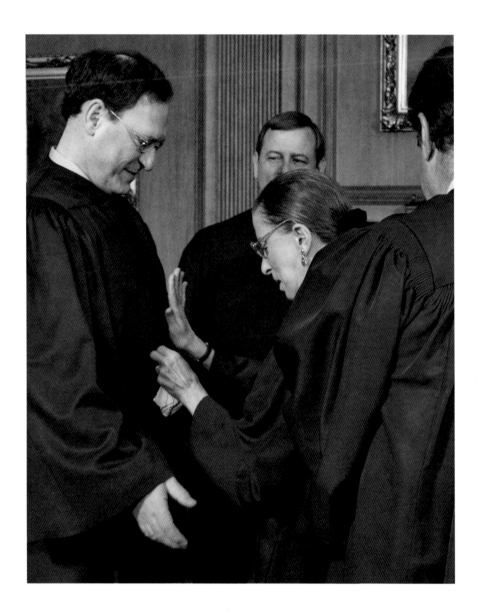

Opposite: (first row, left to right) Justice Antonin Scalia, Justice John Paul Stevens, Chief Justice John G. Roberts, Justice Sandra Day O'Connor, Justice Anthony M. Kennedy, (second row left to right) Justice Ruth Bader Ginsburg, Justice David H. Souter, Justice Clarence Thomas, and Justice Stephen G. Breyer pose at the US Supreme Court the day President George W. Bush nominated Samuel Alito to replace retiring Sandra Day O'Connor, October 31, 2005. **Above**: Justice Ginsburg helps Justice Samuel A. Alito Jr. adjust his robe in the Justices' Conference Room before his formal investiture ceremony, February 16, 2006.

Our Marble Palace

Remarks by Ruth Bader Ginsburg, New England Law, Boston, Massachusetts

March 13, 2009

For these pre-dinner remarks, I have chosen an altogether digestible topic: customs that promote collegiality among the nine justices of the United States Supreme Court. My aim is to describe not the court's heavy work, but the lighter side of life in our marble palace.

I will comment first on our routine gatherings. They begin with handshakes, thirty-six of them to be exact. Before each day in court begins, and before each conference discussion, as we enter the Robing Room or the adjacent conference room, we shake hands, each justice with every other. Every day the court hears arguments, and every day we meet to discuss cases, we lunch together in the justices' dining room. The room is elegant, but the lunch is not haute cuisine. It comes from the court's public cafeteria, the same fare available to anyone who visits the court.

We lunch together by choice, not by rule, usually six to eight of us, and more than occasionally all nine. When Justice O'Connor (currently, the only retired justice) is in town, she often shares the lunch hour with us and enlivens our conversation with reports of her travels in the United States and around the globe.

At the lunch table we may talk about the lawyers' performance in the cases just heard, or a new production in town, perhaps at the DC Shakespeare Theatre or the Washington National Opera, or the latest exhibition at the Library of Congress, National Gallery, or Phillips Collection. Sometimes the younger members of the court speak of their children; the older members, of their grandchildren.

From time to time, we invite a guest to vary the lunch table conversation. Invitees in recent terms have included former secretary of state Condoleezza Rice, former president of the Supreme Court of Israel Aharon Barak, former UN secretary-general Kofi Annan, and, most recently, Albie Sachs, justice of the Constitutional Court of South Africa. (So far, retired Federal Reserve chairman Alan Greenspan and former president of the World Bank Jim Wolfensohn have been our only repeat invitees. Both have an unusual talent. They can engage in lively conversation and eat lunch at the same time.)

We celebrate justices' birthdays with a pre-lunch toast and a "Happy Birthday" chorus generally led by Justice Scalia, because among us, he is best able to carry a tune. Sometimes the celebration includes a cake baked by my husband, master chef and Georgetown University Law Center tax professor Martin D. Ginsburg.

Professor Ginsburg is a regular contributor to the lighter side of life at the Supreme Court. Mainly he performs in the kitchen, for the quarterly spouses lunches held at the court and, occasionally in past years, at a dinner for the entire court family—justices, their spouses, and widows of former Court members. In the beginning, when I was the newest justice, my dear husband offered aid in lightening my load.

During my first months on the court I received, week after week, as I still do, literally hundreds of letters—nowadays increasingly FedExes, faxes, and emails—requesting all manner of responses. Brought up under instructions that plates must be cleaned and communications answered, I was drowning in correspondence despite the best efforts of my resourceful secretaries to contain the flood.

Early in 1994, Justice Scalia and I traveled to India for a judicial exchange. In my absence, my spouse tested his conviction that my mail could be handled more efficiently. He visited chambers, checked the incoming correspondence, grouped the requests into a dozen or so categories, and devised an all-purpose response for my secretaries' signature. When I returned, he gave me the form, which to this day, he regards as a model of utility and grace. I will read a few parts of the letter my husband composed. You may judge for yourself its usefulness and grace.

You recently wrote Justice Ginsburg. She would respond personally if she could, but (as Frederic told Mabel in Gilbert & Sullivan's Pirates of Penzance) *she is not able. Incoming mail reached flood levels months ago and shows no sign of receding.*

To help the Justice stay above water, we have endeavored to explain why she cannot do what you have asked her to do. Please refer to the paragraph below with the caption that best fits your request.

Favorite Recipes. The Justice was expelled from the kitchen nearly three decades ago by her food-loving children. She no longer cooks and the one recipe from her youth, tuna fish casserole, is nobody's favorite.

Photograph. Justice Ginsburg is flattered, indeed amazed, by the number of requests for her photograph. She is now 61 years of age [ah, those were the days!] and understandably keeps no supply.

Are We Related? The birth names of the Justice's parents are Bader and Amster. Many who bear those names have written, giving details of origin and immigration. While the information is engrossing, you and she probably are not related within any reasonable degree of consanguinity. Justice Ginsburg knows, or knew, all of the issue of all in her family fortunate enough to make their way to the U.S.A.

I will spare you my husband's thoughts on fund-raising, school projects, congratulatory letters, document requests, and sundry invitations, and proceed to one last category:

May I Visit? If you are any of the Justice's four grandchildren and wish to visit, she will be overjoyed. If you are a writer or researcher and want to observe the work of Chambers, the answer is "no." Confidentiality really matters in this workplace.

My secretaries, you will not be surprised to learn, vetoed my husband's letter, and in the ensuing years they have managed to cope with the mail flood through measures more *sympathique*.

Since February 5, the day of my pancreatic cancer surgery, messages of hope and offers of prayer have numbered in the hundreds. I have been obliged to respond by a form letter, but this time, it is one I composed.

Returning to the Court's social life, a typical example of events we host every now and then, mainly for lawyers and judges: We take turns greeting attendees at dinners for newly appointed federal judges, gathered in DC for a week of orientation. We also take turns introducing speakers at Supreme Court Historical Society biannual lecture series.

My most recent ventures for the Historical Society involved, first, an October 27 program at

the City Bar Association in New York centered on the work and days of Belva Lockwood, first woman to gain membership in the Supreme Court's Bar. After her 1879 admission, she ran twice for the US presidency, in 1884 and 1888. Next, in December, I presided at a Historical Society sponsored reenactment of the arguments before the Court in a famous case decided in 1908, *Muller v. Oregon*. The Court's decision in *Muller* broke away from the prevailing laissez-faire philosophy and upheld an Oregon law limiting the hours women could be gainfully employed to ten per day. *Muller v. Oregon* is also well known for the brief filed on behalf of Oregon by Louis D. Brandeis. That Brandeis brief contained nearly one hundred pages of real and supposed facts about social and economic conditions, and only a few pages of standard legal argument.

An annual pleasant pause. Each May, just after hearings are over and before the intense end of May, early June weeks when the term's remaining opinions must be completed and released, the court holds a musicale. That tradition was inaugurated in 1988 by Justice Blackmun, who passed the baton to Justice O'Connor when he retired. For the past seven years, I have attended to arrangements for the musicales. We have recently added a fall recital. This term's fall recital artist was Renée Fleming, celebrated diva at the Metropolitan Opera and other grand opera venues around the globe.

In between sitting weeks, some of us spend a day or two visiting US universities or law schools as I am doing just now, or attending meetings with judges and lawyers across the country. Midwinter or summer some of us travel abroad to teach, or to learn what we can about legal systems in distant places. For example, in recent recesses, I have taught, lectured, or participated in meetings of jurists in Australia, Austria, China, England, France, India, Ireland, Israel, Italy, Japan, New Zealand, and South Africa.

Work at the US Supreme Court is ever challenging, enormously time consuming, and tremendously satisfying. We are constantly reading, thinking, and trying to write so that at least lawyers and other judges will understand our rulings.

As you may have noticed, we have sharp differences on certain issues—fairly recent examples include affirmative action, public school desegregation, the death penalty, control of electoral campaign financing, and access to court by detainees in Guantanamo Bay. But through it all, we remain good friends, people who respect each other and genuinely enjoy each other's company. In recent terms, we have even managed to agree, unanimously, some 30 to 40 percent of the time. That contrasts with the court's 5–4 splits, which last term accounted for about 16 percent of the court's decisions. Our mutual respect is only momentarily touched, in most instances, by our sometimes strong disagreements on what the law is.

All of us appreciate that the institution we serve is far more important than the particular individuals who compose the court's bench at any given time. And our job, in my view, is the best work a jurist anywhere could have. Our charge is to pursue justice as best we can. The Founding Fathers were wise enough to equip us to do that by according us life tenure (or, as the Constitution says, tenure "during good behaviour"), and salaries that cannot be diminished while we hold office.

> But through it all, we remain good friends, people who respect each other and genuinely enjoy each other's company.

Our former chief justice, William H. Rehnquist, spoke of the role of the judge using a sports metaphor: "The Constitution has placed the judiciary in a position similar to that of a referee in a basketball game who is obliged to call a foul against a member of the home team at a critical moment in the game: he will be soundly booed, but he is nonetheless obliged to call it as he saw it, not as the home court crowd wants him to call it."

The day any judge shirks from that responsibility, Chief Justice Rehnquist counseled, is the day he or she should resign from office. All members of today's court would concur in that counsel.

With thanks for your patient audience, it is now time to say bon appetit!

Above: An illustration by Art Lien from the 2017 Supreme Court Historical
Society cookbook *Table for Nine: Supreme Court Food Traditions and Recipes*.
Opposite: Riding an elephant with Justice Scalia while taking part in a judicial
exchange in Jaipur, India, 1994. Justice Ginsburg explained to her "feminist
friends" that the seating positions were decided by the elephant driver as a
matter of weight distribution.

Above: RBG swearing in incoming secretary of state Condoleezza Rice,
January 28, 2005. **Opposite**: Addressing the American Civil Liberties
Union Inaugural Membership Conference, Washington, DC, June 2003.

❝ [Justice Scalia] was a jurist of captivating brilliance and wit, with a rare talent to make even the most sober judge laugh . . . It was my great good fortune to have known him as working colleague and treasured friend. ❞

—RBG

Opposite: Members of the US Supreme Court (front to back) John Paul Stevens, Sandra Day O'Connor, Antonin Scalia, Anthony Kennedy, David Souter, Clarence Thomas, Stephen Breyer, and Ruth Bader Ginsburg precede the casket of Chief Justice William Rehnquist on the steps of the US Supreme Court, September 2005. **Above**: Justice Ruth Bader Ginsburg speaking at the memorial service for Justice Antonin Scalia at the Mayflower Hotel in Washington, March 1, 2016.

"It is, as Justice Ginsburg recently put it, 'one of the most exhilarating developments'—a sign of progress that I relish not just as a father who wants limitless possibilities for my daughters, but as an American proud that our Supreme Court will be a little more inclusive, a little more representative, more reflective of us as a people than ever before."

—President Barack Obama

A detail of artist Nelson Shanks's 2012 painting, *The Four Justices*. Top row: (from left) Sonia Sotomayor and Elena Kagan; bottom row: (from left) Sandra Day O'Connor and Ruth Bader Ginsburg.

66 Justice Kennedy assured me that he would keep Justice Kagan out of trouble, and Justice Ginsburg assured me that she would get Justice Kagan into trouble. So we'll see how that works out. **99**

—President Barack Obama

Opposite: Newly confirmed Supreme Court justice Elena Kagan (right) with fellow justice Ginsburg and President Obama in the Blue Room of the White House the day of Kagan's confirmation reception, 2010. **Above**: (from left) Justices Sonia Sotomayor, Ruth Bader Ginsburg, and Elena Kagan in the Justices' Conference Room before Kagan's investiture ceremony, October 1, 2010.

Supreme Court justice Ruth Bader Ginsburg arriving in the House
chambers for President Obama's address to a joint session of Congress,
February 24, 2009, at the US Capitol in Washington, DC.

Supreme Court justices Ruth Bader Ginsburg (left) and Sonia Sotomayor
on their way to the House Chamber for President Barack Obama's State
of the Union address, January 27, 2010. **Following pages**: (from left)
Justices Roberts, Kennedy, Ginsburg, Breyer, Sotomayor, and Kagan at the
State of the Union address on Capitol Hill, February 12, 2013.

An Appeal to the Intelligence of a Future Day

Ruth Bader Ginsburg on the role of disenting opinions [abridged],
Ahavath Achim Synagogue, Atlanta, Georgia

October 21, 2007

Artworks in my chambers display in Hebrew letters the command from Deuteronomy: *Zedek, zedek tirdof*—"Justice, justice shalt thou pursue." These postings serve as ever-present reminders of what judges must do "that they may thrive." In the Supreme Court of the United States, with difficult cases on which reasonable minds may divide, sometimes intensely, one's sense of justice may demand a departure from the majority's view, expressed in a dissenting opinion. This audience, I thought, might find of interest some reflections on the role dissents play in the US judicial system.

Our chief justice, in his confirmation hearings, expressed admiration for the nation's fourth chief justice, John Marshall, in my view, shared by many, the greatest chief justice in US history. Our current chief admired, particularly, Chief Justice Marshall's unparalleled ability to achieve consensus among his colleagues. During his tenure, the court spoke with one voice most of the time.

In Chief Justice Roberts's first year at the helm, which was also Justice O'Connor's last term on our bench, it appeared that the chief's hope for greater unanimity might be realized. In the 2005–2006 term, 45 percent of the cases we took up for review were decided unanimously, with but one opinion for the court, and 55 percent were unanimous in the bottom-line judgment. This past term, however, revealed that predictions of more consensus decision making were off the mark. We spoke with one voice in only 25 percent of the cases presented, and were unanimous in the bottom-line judgment less than 40 percent of the time. Fully one-third of the cases we took up—the highest share in at least a decade—were decided by a bare majority of five.

Typically, when court decisions are announced from the bench, only the majority opinion is summarized. Separate opinions, concurring or dissenting, are noted, but not described. A dissent presented orally therefore garners immediate attention. It signals that, in the dissenters' view, the court's opinion is not just wrong, but importantly and grievously misguided. Last term, a record seven dissents were summarized from the bench, six of them in cases the court decided by 5–4 votes.

I described from the bench two dissenting opinions. The first deplored the court's approval of a federal ban on so-called partial-birth abortion. Departing from decades of precedent, the court placed its imprimatur on an anti-abortion measure that lacked an exception safeguarding a woman's health. Next, I objected to the court's decision making it virtually impossible for victims of pay discrimination to mount a successful Title VII challenge. (Commenting on these orally announced dissents, Linda Greenhouse, the *New York Times*'s star Supreme Court reporter, wrote that last term will be remembered as the one in which I "found [my] voice, and used it." That appraisal surprised my husband, my children, my chambers staff, and even my colleagues at the court. All of them have heard me use my voice, sometimes to stirring effect. But it is true, as Linda Greenhouse knew, that only six times before, in thirteen terms on the Court, and never twice in the same term, did I find it appropriate to underscore a dissent by reading a summary of it aloud in the courtroom.)

Our practice of revealing dissents, it bears emphasis, is hardly universal. In the civil law tradition that holds sway in Europe, and in countries once controlled by a continental power, courts issue a collective judgment, written in an impersonal style. The author of the judgment is neither named nor otherwise identifiable. Disagreement, if it exists, is not disclosed. That pattern prevails without exception in French tribunals, and it is also followed by the European Court of Justice, the high court of the European Union, seated in Luxembourg.

> A dissent presented orally therefore garners immediate attention. It signals that, in the dissenters' view, the court's opinion is not just wrong, but importantly and grievously misguided.

The British common law tradition lies at the opposite pole. In appeals in that tradition, there was conventionally no "opinion for the court" disposing of a case under review. Instead, the judges hearing the matter composed their own individual opinions which, taken together, revealed the court's disposition. Changes in British practice and in some European tribunals have brought these divergent systems closer together. The European Court of Human Rights, for example, seated in Strasbourg, publishes signed dissenting opinions. But, by and large, the historical traditions hold.

Our system occupies a middle ground between the continental and the British patterns.

In the earliest days of our national existence, the US Supreme Court, like the House of Lords, Britain's highest tribunal, issued *seriatim* opinions. Each justice spoke for himself whenever more than a memorandum judgment issued. But John Marshall, who served as chief justice from 1801 until 1835, thought that practice ill advised. In its place, he established the practice of announcing judgments in a single opinion for the court, which he generally wrote himself. Opinions that speak for the court remain the custom today. But unlike courts in civil law systems, and in line with the British tradition, each member of the court has the prerogative to speak out separately.

What is right for one system and society may not be right for another. The civil law–style judgment is suited to a system in which judges train for and embark on career service soon after university graduation. Promotions in such systems generally depend upon the recommendation of longer-tenured, higher-ranking judges. Common law judges, in contrast, are recruited at middle age from the senior ranks of the practicing bar or of law faculties.

In civilian systems, the nameless, stylized judgment and the disallowance of dissent are thought to foster the public's perception of the law as dependably stable and secure. Our tradition, on the other hand, safeguards the independence of the individual judge and prizes the transparency of the process of wielding judicial power.

No doubt, as Chief Justice Roberts suggested, the US Supreme Court may attract greater deference and provide clearer guidance when it speaks with one voice. And I agree that a justice, contemplating publication of a separate writing, should ask himself: is this dissent or concurrence really necessary? Consider the extra weight carried by the court's unanimous opinion in *Brown v. Board of Education*. In that case, all nine justices signed on to one opinion, making it clear that the Constitution does not tolerate legally enforced segregation in our nation's schools. With similar heft, in a follow-up case, *Cooper v. Aaron*, all nine justices jointly authored a statement for the court powerfully reaffirming—in the face of official resistance in Little Rock, Arkansas—that desegregation in public schools is indeed the law of the land.

On the utility of dissenting opinions, I will mention first their in-house impact. My experience teaches that there is nothing better than an impressive dissent to improve an opinion for the court. A well-reasoned dissent will lead the author of the majority opinion to refine and clarify her initial circulation. An illustration: I wrote for the court in the Virginia Military Institute case, which held that VMI's denial of admission to women violated the Equal Protection Clause (see pages 118-19). The published opinion was ever so much better than my first draft, thanks to Justice Scalia's attention-grabbing dissent.

Sometimes a dissent is written, then buried by its author. An entire volume is devoted to the unpublished separate opinions of Justice Brandeis. He would suppress his dissent if the majority made ameliorating alterations or, even if he gained no accommodations, if he thought the court's opinion was of limited application and unlikely to cause real harm in future cases.

On rare occasions, a dissent will be so persuasive that it attracts the votes necessary to become the opinion of the court. I had the heady experience once of writing a dissent for myself and just one other justice that became the opinion of the court from which only two of my colleagues, in the end, dissented.

Are there lasting rifts sparked by sharply worded dissents? Justice Scalia spoke to that question nicely. He said, "I doubt whether any two justices have dissented from one another's opinions any more regularly, or any more sharply, than did my former colleague Justice William Brennan and I. I always considered him, however, one of my best friends on the court, and I think that feeling was reciprocated." The same might be said about my close friendship with Justice Scalia.

Describing the external impact of dissenting opinions, Chief Justice Hughes famously said: "A dissent in a Court of last resort is an appeal . . . to the intelligence of a future day, when a later decision may possibly correct the error into which the dissenting judge believes the court to have been betrayed."

A classic example is Justice Benjamin Curtis's dissent from the court's now notorious 1856 decision in *Dred Scott v. Sandford*. The court held, 7–2, in *Dred Scott* that people of African descent whose ancestors were brought here as slaves could never become American citizens. Justice Curtis disagreed in an opinion remarkable for its time. At the founding of our nation, he wrote, Blacks were "citizens of at least five States, and so in every sense part of the people of the United States," thus "among those for whom and whose posterity the Constitution was ordained and established."

And I agree that a justice, contemplating publication of a separate writing, should ask himself: is this dissent or concurrence really necessary?

Dissents of this order, Justice Scalia rightly commented, "augment rather than diminish the prestige of the Court." He explained: "When history demonstrates that one of the Court's decisions has been a truly horrendous mistake, it is comforting . . . to look back and realize that at least some of the justices saw the danger clearly and gave voice, often eloquent voice, to their concern."

Though Justice Scalia would not agree with me in this further example, I would place Justice Breyer's dissent in last term's school integration cases in

the same category. In those cases, the court invalidated student assignment plans adopted in Seattle, Washington, and Louisville, Kentucky. The plans were designed by the cities' authorities to counter resegregation in the local public schools. The question was whether local communities had leeway to use race-conscious criteria for the purpose of bringing about the kind of racially integrated education *Brown v. Board of Education* anticipated. The court held, 5–4, that the Constitution proscribed Louisville's and Seattle's efforts.

Justice Breyer's exhaustive dissent concluded: "[T]he very school districts that once spurned integration now strive for it. The long history of their efforts reveals the complexities and difficulties they have faced. . . . [T]hey have asked us not to take from their hands the instruments they have used to rid their schools of racial segregation, instruments . . . they believe are needed to overcome the problems of cities divided by race and poverty. . . . The last half-century has witnessed great strides towards racial equality, but we have not yet realized the promise of *Brown*. To invalidate the plans under review is to threaten [*Brown's* promise] . . . This is a decision . . . the Court and the Nation will come to regret."

One of the two dissenting opinions I read from the bench in the 2006–2007 term serves as my last illustration of an appeal "to the intelligence

Opposite: In her chambers at the Supreme Court in Washington, DC, 2013.

> "When history demonstrates that one of the Court's decisions has been a truly horrendous mistake, it is comforting . . . to look back and realize that at least some of the justices saw the danger clearly and gave voice, often eloquent voice, to their concern."—Justice Scalia

of a future day." Seven years ago, the court held Nebraska's ban on so-called partial-birth abortion unconstitutional, in part because it contained no exception safeguarding the health of the woman. Three years later, in a deliberate effort to undo the court's ruling, Congress passed a federal ban on the same procedure, also without a health exception. The federal ban was promptly challenged and found unconstitutional in the lower courts. A Supreme Court, which no longer included Justice O'Connor, held, 5–4, that the federal ban survived review for constitutionality.

I recalled, in my dissent, that the court had repeatedly reaffirmed the state's unconditional obligation, when regulating abortion, to safeguard the woman's health. Not only did the court, last term, refuse to take seriously once solid precedent demanding a health exception, but the majority also—and alarmingly, in my judgment—resurrected "ancient notions about women's place in the family and under the Constitution." Both

107

the federal ban, and the majority's approval of it, I observed, were endeavors "to chip away at a [constitutional] right declared again and again by th[e] Court," and, until the Court's *volte-face*, "with increasing comprehension of its centrality to women's lives." "A decision" of the character the court rendered, I said in conclusion, "should not have staying power."

A well-reasoned dissent will lead the author of the majority opinion to refine and clarify her initial circulation.

I turn now to another genre of dissent, one aiming to attract immediate public attention and to propel legislative change. My example is the second dissent I read from the bench last term. The case involved a woman, Lilly Ledbetter, who worked as an area manager at a Goodyear tire plant in Alabama—in 1997, the only woman in Goodyear to hold such a post. Her starting salary (in 1979) was in line with the salaries of men performing similar work. But over time, her pay slipped. By the end of 1997, there was a 15 to 40 percent disparity between Ledbetter's pay and the salaries of her fifteen male counterparts. A federal jury found it "more likely than not that [Goodyear] paid [Ledbetter] a[n] unequal salary because of her sex." The Supreme Court nullified that verdict, holding that Ledbetter filed her claim too late.

It was incumbent on Ledbetter, the court said, to file charges of discrimination each time Goodyear failed to increase her salary commensurate with the salaries of her male peers. Any annual pay decision not contested promptly (within 180 days), the court ruled, became grandfathered, beyond the province of Title VII (our principal law outlawing employment discrimination) ever to repair.

The court's ruling, I observed for the dissenters, ignored real-world employment practices that Title VII was meant to govern: "Sue early on," the majority counseled, when it is uncertain whether discrimination accounts for the pay disparity you are beginning to experience, and when you may not know that men are receiving more for the same work. (Of course, you will likely lose such a less than fully baked case.) If you sue only when the pay disparity becomes steady and large enough to enable you to mount a winnable case, you will be cut off at the court's threshold for suing too late. That situation, I urged, could not be what Congress intended when, in Title VII, it outlawed discrimination based on race, color, religion, sex, or national origin in our nation's workplaces.

Several members of Congress responded within days after the court's decision was issued. A corrective measure passed the House on July 31, 2007. Senator Kennedy introduced a parallel bill, with twenty-one co-sponsors. The response was just what I contemplated when I wrote: "The ball is in Congress' court . . . to correct [the Supreme]

Court's parsimonious reading of Title VII." But the fate of the proposed legislation has been clouded. On July 27, the administration announced that if the measure "were presented to the President, his senior advisors would recommend that he veto the bill."

> I will continue to give voice to my dissent if, in my judgment, the court veers in the wrong direction when important matters are at stake.

Another type of dissent that may sound an alarm and propel change in the law is one at the intermediate appellate court level. When a judge on a mid-level court writes separately, he or she may persuade other courts at that level, thus creating a conflict among appellate courts in different regions of the country, one that the Supreme Court eventually may resolve. An impressive dissent, even in the absence of a division among intermediate courts, may alert the Supreme Court that an issue is difficult, important, and worthy of the justices' attention.

While I hope that the term now under way will see the Supreme Court less divided than the court was in the 2006–2007 term, I will continue to give voice to my dissent if, in my judgment, the court veers in the wrong direction when important matters are at stake. I stress *important matters*,

because I try to follow Justice Brandeis's counsel. He cautioned that "in most matters it is more important that the applicable rule of law be settled than that it be settled right." One might put in that category an ambiguous provision of a complex statutory regime—the Internal Revenue Code, for example. Justices take comfort in such cases from the knowledge that Congress can amend the provision if it believes the court has gone astray.

On when to acquiesce in the majority's view, and when to take an independent stand, Judge Jerome Frank wrote of the model Brandeis set: "Brandeis was a great institutional man. He realized that . . . random dissents . . . weaken the institutional impact of the Court and handicap it in the doing of its fundamental job. Dissents . . . need to be saved for major matters if the Court is not to appear indecisive and quarrelsome. . . . To have discarded some of [his separate] opinions is a supreme example of [Brandeis's] sacrifice to [the] strength and consistency of the Court. And he had his reward: his shots [were] all the harder because he chose his ground."

In the years I am privileged to serve on the court I hope I will be granted similar wisdom in choosing my ground.

66 Having had the good fortune to serve beside her on both courts, I can attest that her opinions are always thoroughly considered, always carefully crafted, and almost always correct (which is to say we sometimes disagree). That much is apparent for all to see. What only her colleagues know is that her suggestions improve the opinions the rest of us write, and that she is a source of collegiality and good judgment in all our work. 99

—Antonin Scalia

Opposite: Justice Ruth Bader Ginsburg and Justice Antonin Scalia, 2006.
Above: Justices Scalia and Ginsburg appearing on *The Kalb Report* at the
National Press Club in Washington, DC, April 17, 2014.

66 RBG's jabots are a language of their own. The justice
who despises frippery in her writing uses her neck
accessories as a rhetorical flourish. 99

—Irin Carmon and Shana Knizhnik, *Notorious RBG*

Above and **Opposite**: RBG wearing some of the many collars—also known as jabots—she wears with her robes.
Chief Justice John Roberts (opposite, bottom) followed by Associate Justices Anthony Kennedy, Ruth Bader
Ginsburg, and Sonia Sotomayor as they arrive in the House Chamber of the US Capitol to hear an address from
Pope Francis, September 24, 2015. **Following pages**: Supreme Court justices—(from left) Roberts, Kennedy,
Ginsburg, Breyer, Sotomayor, and Kagan—stand and applaud President Barack Obama at the State of the
Union address, January 20, 2015.

Opposite: Wearing one of her favorite jabots, RBG gives President Barack Obama some support as he enters the House Chamber of the Capitol to deliver his State of the Union address, January 28, 2014. **Above**: Justice Ginsburg wears lace gloves paired with a delicately beaded jabot from Cape Town, South Africa—her favorite—to the State of the Union Address as fellow justices (from left) John Roberts, Anthony Kennedy, Stephen Breyer, and Sonia Sotomayor look on, January 25, 2011.

Simply Because They Are Women

United States v. Virginia, *No. 94-1941*, Virginia v. United States, *No. 94-2107*

Bench Announcement

June 26, 1996

This case concerns an incomparable military college, the Virginia Military Institute (VMI), the sole single-sex school among Virginia's public institutions of higher learning. Since its founding in 1839, VMI has produced civilian and military leaders for the commonwealth and the nation. The school's unique program and unparalleled record as a leadership training ground has led some women to seek admission.

The United States, on behalf of women capable of all the activities required of VMI cadets, instituted this lawsuit in 1990, maintaining that under the Equal Protection Clause of the Fourteenth Amendment to the United States Constitution, Virginia may not reserve exclusively to men the educational opportunities that VMI, and no other Virginia school, affords.

The case has had a long history in court.

In the first round, the District Court ruled against the United States, reasoning that the all-male VMI served the State's policy of affording a diverse array of educational programs.

The Fourth Circuit vacated that judgment, concluding that a diversity policy serving to favor one gender did not constitute equal protection.

In the second round, the lower courts considered, and found satisfactory, the remedy Virginia proposed: a program for women, called the Virginia Women's Institute for leadership or VWIL at a private women's college, Mary Baldwin College.

A VWIL degree, the Fourth Circuit said, would not carry the historical benefits and prestige of a VMI degree, and the two programs differed markedly in methodology—VMI's is rigorously "adversative," VWIL's would be "cooperative."

But overall, the lower courts concluded, these schools were sufficiently comparable to meet the demand of equal protection.

We reverse that determination.

Our reasoning centers on the essence of the complaint of the United States, and on facts that are undisputed: Some women, at least, can meet the physical standards VMI imposes on men, are capable of all the activities required of VMI cadets, prefer VMI's methodology over VWIL's, could be educated using VMI's methodology, and would want to attend VMI if they had the chance.

With recruitment, the District Court recognized, VMI could "achieve at least 10 percent female enrollment"—a number, the District Court said, "sufficient . . . to provide female cadets with a positive educational experience."

If most women would not choose VMI's adversative method, many men, too, would not want to be educated in VMI's environment.

The question before us, however, is not whether women or men should be *forced* to attend VMI. Rather, the question is whether Virginia can constitutionally deny to women who have the will and capacity, the training and attendant opportunities VMI uniquely affords—training and opportunities the VWIL program does not supply.

To answer that question, we must have a measuring rod—what lawyers call a standard of review.

In a nutshell, this is the standard our precedent establishes: Defenders of sex-based government action must demonstrate an "exceedingly persuasive justification" for that action. To make that demonstration, the defender of a gender line must show, "at least, that the [challenged] classification serves important governmental objectives and that [any] discriminatory means employed [is] substantially related to the achievement of those objectives."

The heightened review standard applicable to sex-based classification does not make sex a proscribed classification, but it does mark as presumptively invalid—incompatible with equal protection—a law or official policy that denies to women, simply because they are women, equal opportunity to aspire, achieve, participate in, and contribute to society based upon what they can do.

Under this exacting standard, reliance on overbroad generalizations, typically male or typically female "tendencies," estimates about the way most women (or most men) are, will not suffice to deny opportunity to women whose talent and capacity place them outside the average description.

As this court said in *Mississippi University for Women v. Hogan* some fourteen years ago, state actors may not close entrance gates based on "fixed notions concerning the roles and abilities of males and females."

A remedial decree must cure the constitutional violation—in this case, the categorical exclusion of women from an extraordinary educational/leadership development opportunity afforded men.

To cure that violation, and to afford genuinely equal protection, women seeking and fit for a VMI-quality education cannot be offered anything less.

We therefore reverse the Fourth Circuit's judgment, and remand the case for proceedings consistent with this opinion.

The chief justice has filed an opinion concurring in the judgment; Justice Scalia has filed a dissenting opinion. Justice Thomas took no part in the consideration or decision of the case.

———

RBG wrote the majority opinion on VMI, as well as this official summary. Since opinions are long and complicated, the author of the opionon traditionally also writes a distilled version, or "bench announcement," and reads it from the bench.

66 At the time, I was too naïve and sheltered to realize the impact that Justice Ginsburg had on everything and the impact she would have on my life, but I can tell you since then I've been a very quiet but passionate advocate for equal opportunity, not just for women but across the board.99

—Army major Angela Scott, class of 2001

Above: Nichole "Nikki" Harding, a VMI cadet receives her class ring, 2012. **Opposite**: Onstage in Cameron Hall at Virginia Military Institute, Lexington, Virginia, February 1, 2017.

"I went to VMI [Virginia Military Institute] to celebrate the twentieth anniversary of that decision, and it was a joy to see how well it has worked out. They are very proud of their women cadets. These are women who want to be engineers, nuclear scientists. They have women on the faculty now, on their board of directors, and the general, with the agreement of his faculty, told me it's a much better place."

—RBG

Associate Justice Ruth Bader Ginsburg in her chambers at the Supreme Court, July 24, 2013.

123

A court artist's view of former George W. Bush's solicitor general Theodore Olson representing *Citizens United* before the Supreme Court, September 9, 2009. Seated (from left) are Justices Alito, Ginsburg, Kennedy, Stevens, Roberts, Scalia, Thomas, Breyer, and Sotomayor, the court's newest member.

Justices (seated left to right) Breyer, Thomas, Kennedy, Stevens,
Roberts, Scalia, Souter, Ginsburg, and Alito listen to oral arguments
in a lawsuit against tobacco giant Philip Morris, October 31, 2006.

" I spent several months in Sweden in 1962 and 1963, attempting to learn about, and then convey to a common-law bar and bench, the main lines of Sweden's judicial system. . . . In those years I came to appreciate the value of a comparative perspective on the law. An unexpected dividend. Studying about and observing another legal system in operation, I came to understand more completely the United States system in which I was schooled. I became a better teacher of procedure and a better judge, too, I believe, as a result of the experience. "

—RBG

In her Supreme Court chambers, July 2014.

French president Jacques Chirac (center) listens to US Supreme
Court justices (from left) Stephen Breyer, Sandra Day O'Connor, and
Ruth Bader Ginsburg and US ambassador to France Howard H. Leach
(right) in Paris, July 2003.

Justice Ginsburg with Secretary of State Hillary Rodham Clinton
at the State Department before leaving for North Africa to meet
judges and legal scholars and to speak to students at the Cairo
University law school in Egypt, January 2012.

Above: With Senator John McCain at a luncheon in the Capitol's Statuary Hall in honor of President Obama's inauguration, January 20, 2009.
Opposite: Supreme Court justice—and opera buff—Ginsburg at the annual American Bar Association meeting participating in a panel discussion on the lessons operatic performance can bring to the law. At left is US solicitor general Donald Verrilli Jr., Chicago, August 3, 2012.

❝ Justice Ginsburg did not only aim to bend gendered assumptions about women's roles . . . [H]er work sought to undermine the constraints imposed on all persons who were penalized for failing to conform to a social order's expectations. ❞

—Judith Resnik, Yale Law School

Opposite: Discussing *Roe v. Wade* on its fortieth anniversary at the University of Chicago Law School in Chicago, May 11, 2013. **Above**: Onstage at Maria Shriver's Women's Conference in Long Beach, California, 2010.

> " I have memories as a child, even before the war, of being in a car with my parents and passing a place in [Pennsylvania], a resort with a sign out in front that read: 'No dogs or Jews allowed.' Signs of that kind existed in this country during my childhood. "
>
> —RBG

Justice Ginsburg (front row, third from left) listening to President Obama at a Hanukkah reception in the Grand Foyer of the White House. Onstage with him (from left) are Dr. Jill Biden, Vice President Joe Biden, and First Lady Michelle Obama, December 8, 2011.

PART FOUR

LONGEVITY & LEGACY

Full Steam

And then there were two. Then three—four!

Sandra Day O'Connor had been the first and only woman on the Supreme Court for twelve years by the time Ruth joined the bench in 1993. After O'Connor's retirement twelve years later, Ruth was "all alone" for nearly four years until President Barack Obama appointed Sonia Sotomayor in 2009 and Elena Kagan in 2010. With a history of four female justices and a current lineup of three, Ruth remarked that having a trio of women on the court made "an enormous difference. . . . Kagan is on my left, and Sotomayor is on my right. So we look like we're really part of the court and we're here to stay. Also . . . they're not shrinking violets."

In 2018, with a twenty-five-year run on the court, Ruth has no intention of retiring. She is a vigorous justice at eighty-five, even after battling cancer twice and suffering the loss of Marty from cancer in 2010.

After her bout with colon cancer in 1999, when she remarked that she "looked like a survivor of Auschwitz," Ruth began working out twice a week with personal trainer Bryant Johnson, a DC District Court staffer and sergeant in the Army Reserves. Johnson is a key player in Ruth's promise to stay on the bench as long as

Opposite: The Notorious R.B.G., 2014.

possible: "I will do this job as long as I can do it full steam," she vowed in 2017, and by her ability to spend two hours a week repeating bench presses, squats, and pushups, she seems to have plenty of steam left.

The life balance she learned to appreciate in law school may also count for her longevity, as well as her passion for the arts and circle of friends and family. The death of her longtime friend, colleague, and fellow opera lover Antonin Scalia in 2016 was the last act in a friendship that befuddled many. How could the court's seeming opposites—the "intellectual lions of the left and right"—form such a bond? Lisa Blatt, a lawyer who clerked for Ruth and has argued many cases before the Supreme Court, explained: "Both of them simply have huge personalities, love the arts, like to laugh, and are brilliant."

In a case of art imitating life, the unlikely friendship inspired composer and lawyer Derrick Wang to memorialize the couple in a one-act comic opera, *Scalia/Ginsburg: A (Gentle) Parody of Operatic Proportions*, which debuted at a festival in 2015 (see page 159). Ruth's celebrity has a further reach in popular culture, with an ongoing impersonation by *Saturday Night Live*'s Kate McKinnon, children's books, *The RBG Workout* book by her trainer, T-shirts proclaiming "I Dissent" and "Notorious RBG," and tattoos of all stripes worn to express an affection for the liberal icon RBG.

The Notorious RBG phenomenon ignited in 2013 when New York University law student Shana Knizhnik launched a Tumblr blog titled *Notorious R.B.G.* as a "digital tribute" to the justice. Likening the tiny, eighty-something Ruth to rapper Notorious B.I.G. sent the message that Ruth, with her recent heated dissents about affirmative action and Voting Rights Act cases, was a "badass" force to be reckoned with. Ruth welcomes the rock-star treatment and is a self-proclaimed fan of the Tumblr site, visiting it regularly to refresh the stash of RBG T-shirts she keeps on hand to give to friends.

Above: A 2013 caricature of US Supreme Court justice Ruth Bader Ginsburg by cartoonist Chris Ware.

> 66 At an event, the questioner asked Ruth about the significance of reading the dissent from the bench. She sat there in her little fishnet gloves and said, 'That means I am very, very angry.' 99
>
> —Diane Crothers, former Rutgers Law student

In the ultimate homage to Ruth's celebrity, two sets of filmmakers captured her story with films released in 2018 to coincide with her twenty-five years on the court. Betsy West and Julie Cohen crafted a documentary, *RBG*, and Mimi Leder directed a feature film about Ruth and Marty's early life and careers, *On the Basis of Sex*, with a screenplay by Ruth's nephew Daniel Stiepleman.

As of 2018, Ruth's real-life family includes her son, James Ginsburg; her daughter, Jane Ginsburg; her son-in-law, George Spera; and grandchildren Clara and Paul Spera. Law is the family legacy: Jane is a professor at Columbia Law School, Jane's husband is a lawyer with a firm in New York, and their daughter Clara is a recent graduate of Harvard Law now clerking for a federal judge in New York. James, however, took after his mother's love of classical music and launched the multiple-Grammy-winning classical music label Cedille Records.

To Ruth's granddaughter, Clara, the scope of Ruth's achievements and impact did not sink in until she started law school. "It wasn't uncommon for her opinions—or pointed dissents—to be assigned and dissected during class," she said. "I always felt a secret wave of pride and a little awkwardness whenever we discussed her opinions of jurisprudence."

Clara knows that many of her grandmother's fans who sport Notorious RBG T-shirts or tote bags may not be able to name one of her cases, but that's OK. "Instead," she says, "to many, she's a feminist icon because of her tireless persistence at inching us all closer to equality."

Opposite: Justice Ginsburg notes that "the judiciary is not a profession that ranks very high among the glamorously attired," at the *Glamour* Women of the Year Awards in Carnegie Hall, November 12, 2012. **Above**: Georgetown Law School dean William M. Treanor welcomes Justice Ginsburg for a discussion about her life and work at Georgetown Law School in Washington, DC, April 6, 2018. **Following pages**: In Statuary Hall at a Women's History Month reception hosted by Nancy Pelosi in honor of the women of the US Supreme Court, March 18, 2015.

Above: Fans in Salt Lake City pose with a cutout poster of Justice Ginsburg during a rally in celebration of the Supreme Court decision declaring that same-sex couples have a right to marry anywhere in the United States, June 26, 2015.
Opposite: Carrying a tote with her likeness on one side (and a promotion for the book *I Dissent: Ruth Bader Ginsburg Makes Her Mark* on the other), RBG takes the stage to discuss challenges and opportunities confronting public institutions at Georgetown University in Washington, DC, April 27, 2017.

" My mother was very strong about my doing well in school and living up to my potential. Two things were important to her and she repeated them endlessly. One was to 'be a lady,' and that meant conduct yourself civilly, don't let emotions like anger or envy get in your way. And the other was to be independent, which was an unusual message for mothers of that time to be giving their daughters. "

—RBG

"If you want to be a true professional, you will do something outside yourself. Something to repair tears in your community. Something to make life a little better for people less fortunate than you," says Ruth Bader Ginsburg during a talk about a meaningful life at Stanford University, February 6, 2017.

❝ Think of the tremendous fortune I had because I was alive

and a lawyer in the seventies when it became possible for

change to occur. Up until 1970 it was hopeless. ❞

—RBG

Opposite: Justice Ruth Bader Ginsburg tells students at New England Law in Boston
that advice and camaraderie from her fellow justices helped in her fight against
pancreatic cancer, March 13, 2009. **Above**: At lunch with her old friend, Gloria
Steinem (not shown), in the Supreme Court building, discussing their experiences
at the forefront of the women's movement, 2015. **Following pages**: Marrying David
Hagedorn (left) and Michael Widomski shortly after the Supreme Court's decision
to strike down laws denying federal benefits to same-sex spouses, September 2013.

Justice Ginsburg taking part in a panel discussion celebrating her pioneering work to end gender stereotyping and discrimination and establish gender equality during alumni weekend at Yale University, October 2012.

With Vice President Joe Biden (right) and Senator Arlen Specter during an
event honoring Jewish American Heritage Month in the East Room of the
White House, May 27, 2010.

My Career in Opera

Remarks for Chautauqua Institution, Chautauqua, New York

July 29, 2013

I am delighted to be in Chautauqua on a day of two very special events. First, the Pacifica Quartet's recital at four this afternoon. My son, who makes classical CDs, has produced exquisite recordings of the Pacifica playing Mendelssohn and Shostakovich string quartets. The members of the quartet are extraordinarily gifted, energizing, altogether engaging young artists, as those who attend the recital will agree. Second, *Falstaff*, the last opera Verdi composed, will be performed this evening. Verdi was age seventy-nine when he wrote this great work. Verdi loved Shakespeare and, in *Falstaff*, he used Shakespeare's characters to marvelously humorous effect.

My aim this morning is to convey to you why opera is my favorite art form. For over four centuries opera has transported audiences who come, as I do, for the music, the stories, the singers, the drama, or, as *Falstaff* illustrates, the comedy.

I will speak of law and lawyers in opera. My competence to address the topic may not be altogether apparent to you. Truth be told, I am ill-equipped to break out in song. My grade school music teacher ranked me a sparrow, not a robin. The instruction given me: do not sing, only mouth the words. Still, in my dreams, I can be a great diva, often Renata Tebaldi, sometimes Beverly Sills or Marilyn Horne.

My performing career begins and ends at the Washington National Opera, where I have thrice appeared as a super. I debuted in 1994, along with Justice Scalia, in a production of Richard Strauss's *Ariadne auf Naxos*. We were supers again in the same opera in 2009. In between, in 2003, I was onstage in Johann Strauss's *Die Fledermaus*. At Prince Orlofsky's ball in the lush second act of *Fledermaus*, three black-robed justices entered onstage as specially announced guests, billed as "The Supremes." Flanked by Justice Kennedy on one side, Justice Breyer on the other, I had the extraordinary opportunity to hear Plácido Domingo's glorious voice at very close range.

Lawyers and judges, as rule, fare rather badly in operatic works. For positive images there is, perhaps most notably, Moses, Ten Commandments deliverer, treated diversely by Rossini and

Schoenberg. It runs downhill from there. Think of Dr. Blind, the lawyer in *Die Fledermaus*. His ineffective assistance gets for his client, Eisenstein, a few extra days in jail. Or the lawyer in Gershwin's *Porgy and Bess*, who offers Bess a divorce for a dollar, then ups the price to $1.50 when Bess tells him she was never really married before.

In a delightful twenty-first-century comic opera, *Volpone*, music by John Musto, lyrics by Mark Campbell, there is a major role for a lawyer. His name is revealing. He is Voltore (the vulture). The libretto describes Voltore as a baritone, sixty-ish in age, thin and bony, oily hair, scraggly gray beard, posture permanently stooped like a hovering scavenger. Near the end, Voltore is carted off to jail, condemned as a dissembler and thief. He protests, loudly: "Innocent. A man of the law. Innocent. It is an audacity to question my veracity."

Numerous notaries show up in eighteenth- and nineteenth-century operas. They most often oversee the signing of marriage contracts and have few notes to sing.

Chautauqua's invitation challenged me to consider the question anew. I did, and found it fair to say law's part in opera plots is palpable. Trials and inquests abound. A select few: a Revolutionary tribunal condemns the poet Andrea Chénier; in *Aida*, the priests of Phtah condemn Radamès for treason; in *Norma*, the pagan throng lets the high priestess burn for breaking her vow of chastity; in *Billy Budd*, a shipboard court-martial convicts beautiful Billy; in *Peter Grimes*, a lawyer-conducted inquest takes place in the opening scene. Robert Ward recalled the Salem witch trials in retelling with music Arthur Miller's *The Crucible*. Josef K. is tried and executed for an unspecified crime in *Der Prozess*. A trial for murder in apartheid South Africa is staged in *Lost in the Stars*, performed movingly by the Glimmerglass Festival in Cooperstown last summer. In the first act of *Oscar*, an opera by Theodore Morrison that opened in Santa Fe this summer, Oscar Wilde is sentenced to two years of hard labor for "gross indecency." Death administered by the state for a capital crime is portrayed with chilling effect in Jake Heggie's *Dead Man Walking*.

Truth be told, I am ill-equipped to break out in song. My grade school music teacher ranked me a sparrow, not a robin.

Turning to church-state conflict, what scene more powerful than the Grand Inquisitor's confrontation of King Philip in *Don Carlo*. Jails and prisons are settings of choice in grand opera. Prison scenes are staged in *Fidelio*, *Il Trovatore*, *Faust*, *Tosca*, *Dialogues of the Carmelites*, *From the House of the Dead*, *Dead Man Walking*, and scores more. Most recently, in the second act of *Oscar*, Wilde suffers humiliation and cruelty in prison, and writes his last great work, *The Ballad of Reading Gaol*. Carmen is dispatched to jail, but she

Above: Praising a performance of *Carmen* to Washington National Opera artistic director Francesca Zambello and Bryan Hymel (singing as Don José) at the Washington National Opera, 2015.

escapes after negotiating opera's best-known plea bargain.

Wills are plot turners in, among others, *Gianni Schicchi*, the opera in which Woody Allen made his operatic directing debut in 2008, in a Los Angeles Opera production. Once customary law (*le droit de seigneur*; the right of the master to the first night with a servant or peasant bride on his estate) is reluctantly renounced by the Count in *The Marriage of Figaro*.

The eloquence of Daniel Webster is displayed in an opera by Douglas Stuart Moore, based on the Stephen Vincent Benét story *The Devil and Daniel Webster*. Simon Boccanegra pleads for law and order in his resounding act 1 aria "Plebe! Patrizi!" The entire first act of Janacek's *The Makropulous Case* takes place in a lawyer's office. (Dullest act

in the opera, some have said.) A *sympathique* lawyer narrates the unfolding tragedy in William Bolcom's operatic rendition of Arthur Miller's *A View from the Bridge*.

And in an opera premiered at Santa Fe in the summer of 2009, *The Letter* by Paul Moravec, a lawyer faces a moral dilemma. His client has murdered her lover in a fit of jealousy. To gain an acquittal, the lawyer must buy an incriminating letter and suppress its damning contents. (The opera is obviously set in pre–copying machine days, and well before email.)

This highly impressionistic account of law and lawyers in opera should certainly include Wagner's *Ring Cycle*. The Sturm und Drang stem from Wotan's repudiation of the agreement he made to compensate the giants for building Valhalla. What better illustration of the well-known legal maxim *pacta sunt servanda*—in plain English, agreements must be kept. On the lighter side, there is a hilarious scene in *The Marriage of Figaro* in which the

158

ever-resourceful valet escapes the promise of marriage he made to secure a debt he owes to an aging dame, Marcellina.

In light opera, Gilbert and Sullivan's satirical take on the legal system, and the judges and lawyers who populate it, have amused legions of audiences since G&S's first collaboration, in 1875, in *Trial by Jury*.

Chief Justice Rehnquist was a great Gilbert and Sullivan fan. He quoted from both *Trial by Jury* and *Iolanthe* in opinions. And he used as the model for his robe the costume worn by the Lord Chancellor in a low-budget production of *Iolanthe* presented summers ago by a local company in DC. Another Gilbert and Sullivan favorite, *The Pirates of Penzance*, contains the best illustration I know of the distinction between textualist and purposive construction of the law.

Two final comments about opera tied to the Supreme Court. In 1988, Justice Harry Blackmun arranged the first ever afternoon of Music at the Court. Initially, the recitals were held every other year. Under Justice O'Connor's baton after Justice Blackmun retired, the program became an annual event. Since 2002, when I picked up the reins, the event has taken place twice a year. Opera stars who have performed at our recitals include Stephanie Blythe, Renée Fleming, Susan Graham, Denyce Graves, Bryn Terfel, Thomas Hampson, Marcello Giordani, and Samuel Ramey. Instrumentalists include Leon Fleisher and the Pacifica Quartet. The recitals provide a most pleasant pause from the court's heavy occupations. We time the May Musicale just before the pressured late May through June weeks when the justices are consumed with production of all outstanding opinions before the court recesses for the summer.

My finishing note concerns an operatic work in progress. A multitalented composer and June graduate of the University of Maryland Law School, Derrick Wang, is composing a comic opera titled *Scalia/Ginsburg*. Many of the lyrics come from our opinions and speeches. A sample from Justice Scalia's rage aria:

The Justices are blind
How can they spout this—?
The Constitution says absolutely nothing
*   about this!*

And one from my opening aria:

Dear Mister Justice Scalia . . .
You are searching in vain for a bright-line
*   solution*
To a problem that isn't so easy to solve—
But the beautiful thing about our Constitution
Is that, like our society, it can evolve.

The theme: two people with notably different views on constitutional interpretation can nonetheless respect and genuinely like each other. Collegiality of that sort is what makes it possible for the court to do the ever challenging work the Constitution and Congress assign to us, without the fierce partisanship that sometimes mars the operations of the political branches of government.

Previous pages: Justices Ginsburg and Scalia (at center) with Washington National Opera president Robert Craft and his wife, Jamie, in costume for their appearance onstage in the opening night production of *Ariadne auf Naxos* at the Kennedy Center, January 8, 1994. **Above**: At the Harvard University commencement in 2011, Justice Ginsburg was surprised with a serenade from Spanish tenor Plácido Domingo (right). Between them is commencement speaker and honorary degree recipient Ellen Johnson Sirleaf, the president of Liberia. **Opposite**: With an extra from *Carmen* at the Kennedy Center in Washington, DC, September 2015.

Lolo Sarnoff, founder of Arts for the Aging, with her friend Supreme Court justice Ruth Bader Ginsburg at the annual Opera Ball held at the British Embassy in Washington, June 2004.

(from left) American soprano Renée Fleming, Honorable Ruth Bader
Ginsburg, and Barry Tucker, president of the Richard Tucker Music
Foundation at the foundation's thirty-eighth annual gala in Avery Fisher
Hall, New York City, November 17, 2013.

> "She's quite deceiving. She comes in a teeny, tiny package, but she's quite formidable. A real powerhouse and a mighty force to be reckoned with."

—Denyce Graves, American mezzo-soprano

"And finally, after four centuries of delay in seeking payment, we think that Shylock is out of time in asking for interest," decrees Justice Ginsburg while presiding over a mock trial at a performance—which included her grandson, Paul Spera—of Shakespeare's *The Merchant of Venice* at the Scuola Grande di San Rocco in Venice, Italy, July 27, 2016.

167

Above: Kate McKinnon as Supreme Court justice Ruth
Bader Ginsburg on *Saturday Night Live*, November 12, 2016.
Opposite: A display of Justice Ruth Bader Ginsburg coffee mugs
for sale at the Fishs Eddy store on Broadway in New York City.

RUTH BADER
GINSBURG
MUG
$12.95

Ruth Bader Ginsburg
Herstory in the making!

POLITICIAN
MUG SHOTS

66 I celebrated my third birthday at the Supreme Court, just two short months after Bubbie took her oath. I realize now that my birthday party wasn't held there to show off or because the court's such an impressive space; it was because she wanted me to know, from the age of three, that my grandmother, my Bubbie, worked there, and that I shouldn't consider anything out of my reach. 99

—Clara Spera, RBG's granddaughter

Opposite: Waiting with her grandson, Paul Spera, and his friend, Audrey Bastien, at the Santa Fe Opera, 2013. **Above**: A scene with granddaughter, Clara Spera, from the 2018 documentary *RBG*.

“ The whole time that I've trained the justice, the one word she has never used with me is 'can't.' Even when I told her we were going to do push-ups—she looked me with a side-eye, like maybe I was locked on stupid and stuck on dumb. But she didn't say anything. And when Justice Ginsburg finally did push-ups off her knees, she lit up. ”

—Bryant Johnson, personal trainer

Above: RBG with personal trainer, Bryant Johnson, doing her workout in the 2018 documentary *RBG*. **Opposite**: Justice Ginsburg's personal trainer, Bryant Johnson—who also trains Justices Breyer and Kagan—with his book, *The RBG Workout: How She Stays Strong . . . and You Can Too*, October 2017.

66 For Ruth, an ideal version of a movie about her life was to recognize that whatever she has accomplished was on the shoulders of the women who came before her. 99

—Daniel Stiepleman

Stills from the 2018 feature film *On the Basis of Sex*, the story of Ruth Bader Ginsburg, her struggles for equal rights, and what she had to overcome in order to become a US Supreme Court justice. **Opposite**: Harvard Law School student Ruth Bader Ginsburg (Felicity Jones). **Above**: (from left to right) Marty Ginsburg (Armie Hammer), the ACLU's Mel Wulf (Justin Theroux), and Ruth (Felicity Jones) enter a Denver courthouse as co-counsels in the 1972 landmark case of *Moritz v. Commissioner of Internal Revenue*, which resulted in the judgment that the government could not deny benefits to a citizen solely on the basis of sex. Justice Ginsburg supported and approved the script, which was conceived and written by her nephew Daniel Stiepleman.

14th Amendment
No state shall make or enforce any law which shall
of the citizens of the United States; nor shall
life, liberty, or
ty, without due process of
within its
the equal protection of

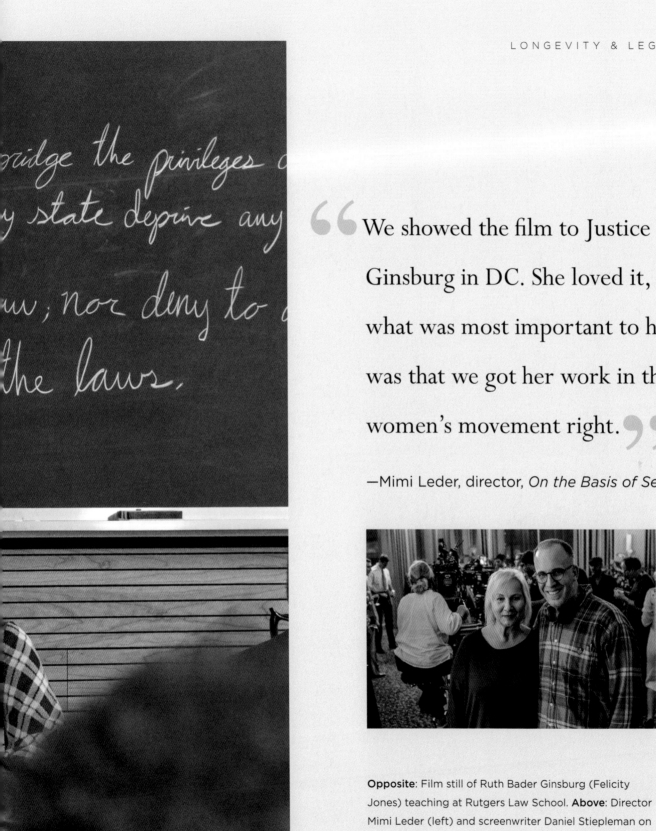

> " We showed the film to Justice Ginsburg in DC. She loved it, and what was most important to her was that we got her work in the women's movement right. "

—Mimi Leder, director, *On the Basis of Sex*

Opposite: Film still of Ruth Bader Ginsburg (Felicity Jones) teaching at Rutgers Law School. **Above**: Director Mimi Leder (left) and screenwriter Daniel Stiepleman on the set of *On the Basis of Sex*.

177

WIRE-RIMMED
GLASSES
TO SEE THROUGH
PATRIARCHAL
BULLSH*T

PULLED-BACK
HAIR
BECAUSE HEROES
HAVE NO TIME FOR
FLYAWAYS

SILK
GLOVES
TO UPHOLD RIGHTS
FOR EVERYONE

ICONIC
JABOT
TO MAKE FASHION
AND JUDICIAL
STATEMENTS

HARDWOOD
GAVEL
TO BRING "ORDER"
TO YOUR LIFE

POINTING
FINGER
TO STEADY THE
SCALES OF JUSTICE

RIGHTEOUS
ROBE
THE NEXT BEST
THING TO A CAPE

HEELED
LOAFERS
TO STAND TALL
AGAINST OPPRESSORS

Above: 2015 RBG tattoo by Washington, DC, tattoo artist Nikki "Balls" Lugo. **Left:** Infographic for the RBG action figure by FCTRY.com from their 2018 Kickstarter campaign. **Opposite:** Stacy Innerst's illustration for the *New York Times* Best Illustrated Children's Books of 2017 award winner *Ruth Bader Ginsburg: The Case of R.B.G. vs. Inequality.*

> **"I think that the most important thing I have done is to enable Ruth to do what she has done."**
>
> —Martin Ginsburg

Justice Stevens and Martin Ginsburg look on as Justice Sonia Sotomayor greets Justice Ruth Bader Ginsburg at the conclusion of a reception honoring Sotomayor as the newest member of the court in the East Room of the White House, August 12, 2009.

Opposite and **Above** and **Following pages**: The Annual Women's History Month reception hosted by Democratic House leader Nancy Pelosi in Statuary Hall on Capitol Hill in Washington, DC, March 18, 2015.

Two hundred candidates from fifty-nine countries are administered
the Oath of Allegiance for US citizenship by Justice Ginsburg at the
New-York Historical Society, April 10, 2018.

"At my age, you have to take it year by year. This year, I'm okay,"
RBG tells the crowd at Temple Emanu-El Skirball Center in New
York, September 21, 2016.

187

Fellow Americans

Remarks by Ruth Bader Ginsburg, New-York Historical Society, New York

April 10, 2018

My fellow Americans, it is my great privilege to welcome you to citizenship in the democracy that is the USA. Today, you join more than twenty million current citizens, born in other lands, who chose, as you have, to make the United States of America their home. We are a nation made strong by people like you who traveled long distances, overcame great obstacles, and made tremendous sacrifices—all to provide a better life for themselves and their families. My own father arrived in this land at age thirteen, with no fortune and speaking no English. My mother was born four months after her parents, with several children in tow, came by ship to Ellis Island. My father and grandparents reached, as you do, for the American dream. As testament to our nation's promise, the daughter and granddaughter of these immigrants sits on the highest court in the land and will proudly administer the oath of citizenship to you.

You have studied our system of government and know of its twin pillars. First, our government has limited powers; it can exercise only the authority expressly given to it by the Constitution. And second, citizens of this country enjoy certain fundamental rights. Those rights are our nation's hallmark and pride. They are set forth in the Bill of Rights, and other amendments to the Constitution. They are inalienable, yielding to no governmental decree. And our Constitution opens with the words "We the people of the United States." By limiting government, specifying rights, and empowering the people, the founders of the USA proclaimed that the heart of America would be its citizens, not its rulers.

After the words "We the people of the United States," the Constitution sets out the aspiration "to form a more perfect Union." At the start, it is true, the union very much needed perfection. The original Constitution permitted slavery and severely limited who counted among "We the people." When the nation was new, only white property-owning men had the right to vote, the most basic right of citizenship. But over the course of our history, people left out at the start—people held in human bondage, Native Americans, and women (50 percent of the population) came to be embraced as full citizens. A French observer of early America, Alexis de Tocqueville, wrote that "The greatness of America lies not in being more enlightened than . . . other nation[s], but rather in her ability to repair her faults." Through amendments to our Constitution, and court decisions applying those amendments, we abolished slavery, prohibited racial discrimination, and made men and women people of equal citizenship stature.

In the vanguard of those perfections were citizens just like you—new Americans of every race and creed, making ever more vibrant our national motto: *e pluribus unum*— out of many, one.

Though we have made huge progress, the work of perfection is scarcely done. Many stains remain. In this rich land, nearly a quarter of our children live in deep poverty, nearly half of our citizens do not vote, and we still struggle to achieve greater understanding and appreciation of each other across racial, religious, and socioeconomic lines. Yet we strive to realize the ideal—to become a more perfect union. As new, well-informed citizens, you will play a vital part in that endeavor by voting in elections, serving on juries, and engaging in civic discourse.

We sing of America as "sweet land of liberty." Newcomers to our shores, people like you, came here from the earliest days of our nation to today, "[seeking] liberty—freedom from oppression, freedom from want, freedom to be [you and me]." I would like to convey to you, finally, how a great American jurist—Judge Learned Hand— understood liberty. He explained in 1944 what liberty meant to him when he greeted a large assemblage of new Americans gathered in Central Park to swear allegiance to the United States. These are Judge Hand's words:

> Just what is this sacred liberty that "must li[e] in the hearts of men and women? It is not the ruthless, the unbridled will; it is not freedom to do as one likes. . . . I cannot define [the spirit of liberty]; I can only tell you my own faith. The spirit of liberty is the spirit which is not too sure that it is right; the spirit of liberty is the spirit which seeks to understand the minds of other men and women; the spirit of liberty is the spirit which weighs their interest alongside its own without bias."

May the spirit of liberty, as Judge Hand explained it, be your beacon. May you have the conscience and courage to act in accord with that high ideal as you play your part in helping to achieve a more perfect union.

"I think Ruth is better at getting along with people with whom we profoundly disagree. I feel invisible in their presence because I'm being treated as invisible. But what we want in the future will only happen if we do it every day. So, kindness matters enormously. And empathy."

—Gloria Steinem

Gloria Steinem lunching with her old friend Justice Ruth Bader Ginsburg at the Supreme Court building Washington, DC, October 28, 2015.

Above: Supreme Court justice Ruth Bader Ginsburg at the inauguration of President
Donald Trump, January 20, 2017. **Opposite**: In an interview with Kenneth Feinberg at
the Washington Hilton, Justice Ginsburg discusses President Trump, the nine-month-
old Supreme Court vacancy, and her nickname, Notorious RBG, inspired by fellow
Brooklynite, the Notorious B.I.G., November 14, 2016.

" The controversies that come to the Supreme Court, as the last judicial resort, touch and concern the health and well-being of our nation and its people. They affect the preservation of liberty to ourselves and our posterity. Serving on this court is the highest honor, the most awesome trust, that can be placed in a judge. "

—RBG

Associate Supreme Court justice Ruth Bader Ginsburg arrives for President Barack Obama's address to a joint session of Congress, February 24, 2009.

Acknowledgments

Sterling Publishing is grateful to Esther Margolis of Newmarket Publishing Management Corporation, who brought us the excellent idea of making this book about Justice Ruth Bader Ginsburg and seamlessly helped to produce it with an excellent team of colleagues and contributors. Newmarket wishes to acknowledge and thank the following:

Acclaimed biographer Antonia Felix, whose insightful text and adept curation of RBG's life provides new twists and turns in our country's struggle for equal rights; Diane Crothers, for her generous time and insights—her distinguished life work in women's rights and social justice advocacy make her a legend in her own right.

At Night & Day Design, the exceptionally talented and unflappable designer Timothy Shaner, and the resourceful, imaginative photo editor and researcher Christopher Measom, whose stunning design, photo selection, and editing delivered these inspiring pages.

The equitable Patricia McCabe Estrada of the Supreme Court, the operatic Sabrina Skacan of the Kennedy Center, the generous Erin Harris from the Avedon Foundation, and the scholarly duo of Sabrina Sondhi at the Columbia Library and Lesley Schoenfeld at the Harvard Library for their help in unearthing some sensational images.

Participant Productions' David Linde, Lynn Hirschfield, Christina Kounelias, and Jamie Cornejo; and Focus Features' Elaine Patterson and Caitlyn Nguyen for their assistance with materials relating to the documentary *RBG* and/or the feature film *On the Basis of Sex*. Special thanks go to the latter's producer, Robert W. Cort, and screenwriter, Daniel Stiepleman.

Very special gratitude goes to Mimi Leder, director of *On the Basis of Sex*, for contributing the book's personal, inspiring foreword.

And at Sterling Publishing, thanks to Lorie Pagnozzi, art director, interiors; Elizabeth Lindy, senior art director, covers and cover designer; Chris Bain, photography director; Fred Pagan, production manager; and finally to executive editor Barbara Berger, whose enthusiasm and expert guidance helped to bring everything together beautifully.

Notes

INTRODUCTION

Page 1: "They think the women's movement": Diane Crothers, interview with the author, June 5, 2018. "Women were only 4 percent": Cynthia Grant Bowman, "Women in the Legal Profession from the 1920s to the 1970s: What Can We Learn from Their Experience about Law and Social Change?" *Maine Law Review* 61, no. 1 (2009): 15, and American Bar Association, "A Current Glance at Women in the Law 2017," americanbar.org/women. "Working as a research assistant": Ruth Bader Ginsburg, Mary Hartnett, and Wendy W. Williams, *My Own Words* (New York: Simon & Schuster, 2016), 21.

Page 2: "repair tears in your community": Kathleen J. Sullivan, "U.S. Supreme Court Justice Ruth Bader Ginsburg Talks about a Meaningful Life," *Stanford News*, February 6, 2017. "who cared that I had a brain": Elahe Izadi, "Ruth Bader Ginsburg's Advice on Love and Leaning In," *Washington Post*, July 31, 2014. "She seemed to have a natural": David Margolick, "Trial by Adversity Shapes Jurist's Outlook," *New York Times*, June 25, 1993. "One of the things": Diane Crothers, interview with the author, June 5, 2018. "Be a lady": Jane Pauley, "Ruth Bader Ginsburg: Her View from the

Bench," CBS News, October 9, 2016. "Celia was the first child": Teri Kanefield, *Free to Be Ruth Bader Ginsburg: The Story of Women and Law* (San Francisco: Armon, 2016), 3.

Page 3: "If I could have any talent": Yvonne S. Lee, "Supreme Performance: Justices Take Stage at Opera," CNN, September 7, 2003. "What is the difference": "Remarks by Ruth Bader Ginsburg," National Commemoration of the Days of Remembrance, US Capitol Rotunda, April 22, 2004. "It seemed to me": "At the U.S. Supreme Court: A Conversation with Justice Ruth Bader Ginsburg," *Stanford Lawyer*, November 11, 2013. "was to root out the gender-based": ibid. "I didn't change the Constitution": "Justice Ginsburg Offers Insights on Legal Questions, Women's Role in Law," "The Takeaway," Public Radio International, September 16, 2003.

Page 4: "to reflect the talent": Ashley Alman, "Ruth Bader Ginsburg Answers the One Question She Loves Being Asked," *Huffington Post*, September 9, 2015. "flaming feminist litigator": Max Greenwood, "Ginsburg Calls Herself a 'Flaming Feminist Litigator,'" *The Hill*, September 20, 2017. "My daughter-in-law": Diane Crothers, interview with the author, June 5, 2018.

PART ONE: ORIGINS

Page 9: **"Named Joan Ruth Bader":** Ronald Collins, Ask the Author: Justice Ginsburg in Her Own Words . . . and Then Some," SCOTUSblog, December 22, 2016. **"kicky baby":** Ginsburg, Hartnett, and Williams, *My Own Words*, 3.

Page 10: **"weekend performance series":** Lucy McCalmont, "Ginsburg Gets Ready for Her Close-up," *Politico*, October 21, 2014. **"riveted by":** Louise T. Guinther, "Liner Notes: Ruth Bader Ginsburg," *Opera News*, April 2017. **"gorgeous music":** Marisa M. Kashino, "Stage Presence: Ruth Bader Ginsburg's Love of the Arts," *Washingtonian*, October 10, 2012. **"the smell of death":** David Von Drehle, "Conventional Roles Hid a Revolutionary Intellect," *Washington Post*, July 18, 1993.

Page 11: **"The Ginsburg marriage was":** Nina Totenberg, "Martin Ginsburg's Legacy: Love of Justice," National Public Radio, July 3, 2010. **"As he would later put it":** Ibid.

Page 16: **"Marty was an extraordinary person":** Irin Carmon, "Ruth Bader Ginsburg on Marriage, Sexism, and Pushups," MSNBC, February 17, 2015.

Page 18: **"That's my dream":** Stephanie Francis Ward, "Family Ties," *ABA Journal*, October 2010.

Page 21: **"My success in law school":** Ruth Bader Ginsburg, "Ruth Bader Ginsburg's Advice for Living," *New York Times*, October 1, 2016.

Page 23: **"Work-life balance was":** Ibid.

Page 30: **"When I announced her appointment":** "Remarks with Judge Ruth Bader Ginsburg and an Exchange with Reporters," US Government Publishing Office, August 3, 1993, p. 1542.

Page 32: **"I have had more than":** Ruth Bader Ginsburg, "Ruth Bader Ginsburg's Advice for Living," *New York Times*, October 1, 2016.

Page 38: **"We had nearly two":** Nina Totenberg, "Martin Ginsburg's Legacy: Love of Justice," National Public Radio, July 3, 2010.

Page 41: **"It takes women and men":** Stephanie Francis Ward, "Family Ties," *ABA Journal*, October 2010.

PART TWO: BREAKING BARRIERS

Page 37: **"one of only nine female students":** Ginsburg, Hartnett, and Williams, *My Own Words*, xx.

Page 38: **"In the fifties":** Tez Clark, "Notorious RBG: Ruth Bader Ginsburg's Journey from ACLU Lawyer to Pop Culture Icon," *Vox*, June 29, 2015. **"became the second female law professor":** Kanefield, *Free to Be Ruth Bader Ginsburg*, 56. **"'separate spheres' mentality":** Alanna Vagianos, "Ruth Bader Ginsburg Tells Young Women: 'Fight for the Things You Care About,'" *Huffington Post*, June 2, 2015.

Page 39: **"legally enforced second-class":** Wendy W. Williams, "Ruth Bader Ginsburg's Equal Protection Clause: 1970–80," *Columbia Journal of Gender and Law* 25 (2013): 42. **"the days of assuming":** Linda Hirshman, *Sisters in Law: How Sandra Day O'Connor and Ruth Bader Ginsburg Went to the Supreme Court and Changed the World* (New York: HarperCollins, 2015), 44. **"She's sort of a steel butterfly":** Linda P. Campbell and Linda M. Harrington, "Ruth Bader Ginsburg: Portrait of a 'Steel Butterfly,'" *Chicago Tribune*, June 27, 1993.

Page 43: **"I was terribly nervous":** Sandra Pullman, "Tribute: The Legacy of Ruth Bader Ginsburg and WRP Staff," American Civil Liberties Union https://www.aclu.org/other/tribute-legacy-ruth-bader-ginsburg-and-wrp-staff.

Page 48: **"I was trying to educate":** Ruth Bader Ginsburg, Senate Judiciary Committee Hearings on Nomination to the Supreme Court (July 20–23, 1993), 122.

Page 66: **"Generally, change in":** Ibid.

PART THREE: MAKING HER CASE

Page 71: **successfully argued five out of six:** David Von Drehle, "Conventional Roles Hid a Revolutionary Intellect, *Washington Post*, July 18, 1993.

Page 72: **"familiar stereotype":** Dahlia Lithwick, "The Mother of All Grizzlies," Slate, August 30, 2010. **"reputation as a moderate judge":** Paul Richter, "Clinton Picks Moderate Judge Ruth Ginsburg for High Court," *Los Angeles Times*, June 15, 1993. **"He wasn't just a great chef":** "Cinema Café with Justice Ruth Bader Ginsburg and Nina Totenberg," video, Sundance Institute, January 21, 2018, https://www.youtube.com/watch?v=pDXxsRB4s7Y.

Page 73: **"One of her favorite things":** Stephanie Francis Ward, "Family Ties," *ABA Journal*, October 2010. **"The court, I fear":** *Burwell v. Hobby Lobby Stores, Inc.,* Opinion, SCOTUSblog.com, June 30, 2014. **"We are not experiencing the best times":** Erin Reimel, "Justice Ruth Bader Ginsburg: 'There Is Reason to Hope That We Will See a Better Day," *Glamour*, February 25, 2017.

Page 77: **"It is true":** Ruth Bader Ginsburg, "Speech to the American Sociological Association Annual Meeting," Montreal, August 11, 2006.

Page 78: **"When I began":** Ruth Bader Ginsburg and Barbara Flagg, "Some Reflections on the Feminist Legal Thought of the 1970's," University of Chicago Legal Forum 1989, no. 1, article 3, 9.

Page 93: **"[Justice Scalia] was a jurist":** Daniel Politi, "Read Justice Ruth Bader Ginsburg's Touching Statement on Scalia," *Slate*, February 14, 2016.

Page 94: **"It is, as Justice Ginsburg":** "Remarks by the President and Elena Kagan at Reception Honoring Her Confirmation," White House, August 6, 2010.

Page 97: **"Justice Kennedy assured":** Ibid.

Page 111: **"Having had the good":** Antonin Scalia, "Ruth Bader Ginsburg," *Time*, April 16, 2015.

Page 112: **"RBG's jabots":** Irin Carmon and Shana Knizhnik, *Notorious RBG: The Life and Times of Ruth Bader Ginsburg* (New York: Dey Street/HarperCollins, 2015), 160.

Page 120: **"At the time":** Jessie Knadler, "Justice Ginsburg Speaks at VMI, an Institute She Transformed," January 31, 2017.

Page 123: **"I went to VMI":** Supreme Court Justice Ruth Bader Ginsburg in Conversation with Charlie Rose, video, 92nd Street Y, September 26, 2017, http://92yondemand.org/supreme-court-justice-ruth-bader-ginsburg-conversation-charlie-rose.

Page 126: **"I spent several months":** Ruth Bader Ginsburg, "Remarks for Suffolk Law School," January 26, 2007.

Page 133: **"Justice Ginsburg did":** Judith Resnik, "Opening the Door: Ruth Bader Ginsburg, Law's Boundaries, and the Gender of Opportunities," Yale Law School Faculty Scholarship Series, paper 4942 (2013), 84.

Page 134: **"I have memories":** Ruth Bader Ginsburg, Senate Judiciary Committee Hearings on Nomination to the Supreme Court (July 20–23, 1993), 139.

PART FOUR: LONGEVITY & LEGACY

Page 139: **"an enormous difference":** Jessica Weisberg, "Supreme Court Justice Ruth Bader Ginsburg: I'm Not Going Anywhere," *Elle*, September 23, 2014. **"looked like a survivor":** Roxanne Roberts, "Read This: The Ruth Bader Ginsburg Workout Plan," *Washington Post*, March 20, 2013.

Page 140: **"I will do this job":** Alex Johnson, "Ruth Bader Ginsburg Signals She'll Stay on Supreme Court as Long as She Can," NBC News, February 23, 2017. **"intellectual lions":** David S. Savage,

"BFFs Ruth Bader Ginsburg and Antonin Scalia Agree to Disagree," *Los Angeles Times*, June 22, 2015. **"Both of them simply have"**: Ibid. **"The Notorious RBG phenomenon ignited in 2013"**: Dahlia Lithwick, "Justice LOLZ Grumpycat Notorious R.B.G.," *Slate*, March 16, 2016.

Page 141: "At an event": Diane Crothers, interview with the author, June 5, 2018. **"It wasn't uncommon"**: Clara Spera, "Ruth Bader Ginsburg's Granddaughter: 'You Know Her as the Notorious RBG, but She's Bubbie to Me,'" *Glamour*, May 4, 2018. **"Instead, to many"**: Ibid.

Page 143: "the judiciary is not": Margaret Wheeler Johnson, "Glamour Women of the Year Awards Honor Ruth Bader Ginsburg, Lena Dunham, Zaha Hadid, and Others," *Huffington Post*, November 13, 2012.

Page 148: "My mother was very strong": Ginsburg, Hartnett, and Williams, *My Own Words*, 5. **"If you want to be"**: Kathleen J. Sullivan "U.S. Supreme Court Justice Ruth Bader Ginsburg Talks about a Meaningful Life," *Stanford News*, February 6, 2017.

Page 151: "Think of the tremendous": Supreme Court Justice Ruth Bader Ginsburg in Conversation with Charlie Rose, video, 92nd Street Y, September 26, 2017, http://92yondemand.org/supreme-court-justice-ruth-bader-ginsburg-conversation-charlie-rose.

Page 167: "She's quite deceiving": Barbara Harrison, "Celebrated Singer, 'Notorious' Supreme Court Justice Bond through Opera."

NBC Washington, March 6, 2017. **"And finally, after four"**: Rachel Donadio, "Justice Ruth Bader Ginsburg Presides over Shylock's Appeal," *New York Times*, July 27, 2016.

Page 171: "I celebrated my": Clara Spera, "Ruth Bader Ginsburg's Granddaughter: 'You Know Her as the Notorious RBG, but She's Bubbie to Me,'" *Glamour*, May 4, 2018.

Page 172: "The whole time": Melena Ryzik, "Ninja Supreme Court Justice: Ruth Bader Ginsburg Has Fun with Fame," *New York Times*, May 9, 2018.

Page 175: "For Ruth, and": Focus Features Q&A with screenwriter.

Page 177: "We showed the film": Focus Features Q&A with director.

Page 180: "I think that the most important": Nina Totenberg, "Martin Ginsburg's Legacy: Love of Justice," National Public Radio, July 3, 2010.

Page 187: "At my age, you have": Valentina Zarya, "If You Could Do As Many Push-ups As Ruth Bader Ginsburg, You Wouldn't Retire Either," *Fortune*, September 22, 2016.

Page 191: "I think Ruth is better at": Philip Galanes, "Ruth Bader Ginsburg and Gloria Steinem on the Unending Fight for Women's Rights," *New York Times*, November 14, 2015.

Page 194: "The controversies that come": Ruth Bader Ginsburg, Senate Judiciary Committee Hearings on Nomination to the Supreme Court (July 20–23, 1993), 51.

Image Credits